MICRO-COSMOGRAPHIE

MICRO-COSMOGRAPHIE OR, A PIECE OF THE WORLD DISCOVERED; IN ESSAYES AND CHARACTERS. BY JOHN EARLE.

PRINTED FROM THE SIXTH AUGMENTED EDITION OF MDCXXXIII AT THE UNIVERSITY PRESS, CAMBRIDGE, & PUBLISHED AT THE CAMBRIDGE UNIVERSITY PRESS WAREHOUSE, AVE MARIA LANE, LONDON, E.C. MDCCCCIII.

TO THE READER.

I HAVE (for once) adventur'd to play the mid-wifes part, helping to bring forth these Infants into the world, which the Father would have smoothered: who having left them lapt up in loose Sheets, as soone as his Fancy was delivered of them, written especially for his private recreation, to passe away the time in the Country and by the forcible request of Friends drawne him; Yet passing severally from hand to hand in written Copies, grew at length to be a pretty number in a little Volume: and among so many sundry dispersed Transcripts, some very imperfect & surreptious, had like to have past the Presse, if the Author had not used speedy meanes of prevention: When perceiving the hazzard he ranne to bee wrong'd, was unwillingly willing to let them passe as now they appeare to the World. If any faults have escap't the Presse, (as few Bookes can bee printed without) impose

them not on the Author, I intreat Thee;
but rather impute them to mine and the
Printers oversight, who seriously promise
on the Re-impression hereof, by greater care
and diligence for this our former default,
to make Thee ample satisfaction. In the
meane while, I remaine,

Thine,

ED. BLOVNT.

A TABLE OF CONTENTS.

x

FINIS.

MICRO-COSMOGRAPHIE

Or,
A Piece of the World
Characteriz'd.

1. A CHILD

IS a Man in a smal Letter, yet the best
Copy of Adam before hee tasted of Eve or the
Apple; & hee is happy, whose small practice
in the world can onely write his Character.
Hee is natures fresh picture newly drawne
in Oyle, which time and much handling
dimmes and defaces. His soule is yet a
white paper unscribled with observations of
the world, wherewith at length it becomes a
blurr'd Note-booke. He is purely happy,
because he knowes no evill, nor hath made
meanes by sinne, to be acquainted with

misery. He arrives not at the mischiefe of being wise, nor endures evils to come by foreseeing them. He kisses and loves all, & when the smart of the rod is past, smiles on his bearer. Nature & his Parents alike dandle him, and tice him on with a bait of Sugar, to a draught of Worme-wood. He playes yet, like a young Prentice the first day, and is not come to his taske of melancholy. All the language he speaks yet, is Teares, and they serve him well enough to expresse his necessity. His hardest labour is his tongue, as if he were loth to use so deceitfull an Organ; & he is best company with it, when hee can but prattle. Wee laugh at his foolish sports, but his game is our earnest: and his Drums, Rattles and Hobby-horses, but the Emblems, and mocking of mens businesse. His father hath writ him as his owne little story, wherein hee reads those dayes of his life that hee cannot remember; and sighes to see what innocence he ha's outliv'd. The elder he growes, hee is a staire lower from God; and like his first father, much worse in his breeches. He is the Christians example, and the old mans relapse: The one imitates his purenesse, & the other falls into his simplicitie. Could hee put off his body with his little

Coate, he had got eternity without a burthen, and exchang'd but one Heaven for
another.

2. A YOUNG RAW PREACHER

IS a Bird not yet fledg'd, that hath hopt
out of his nest to bee Chirping on a hedge,
and will bee stragling abroad at what perill
soever. His backwardnesse in the Vniversitie hath set him thus forward; for had hee
not truanted there, hee had not beene so
hastie a Divine. His small standing and
time hath made him a proficient onely in
boldnesse, out of which & his Table-booke
he is furnisht for a Preacher. His collections of Studie are the notes of Sermons,
which taken up at St. Maries, hee utters in
the Country. And if he write Brachigraphy,
his stocke is so much the better. His writing is more then his reading; for hee reades
onely what hee gets without booke. Thus
accomplisht he comes downe to his friends,
and his first salutation is grace and peace
out of the Pulpit. His prayer is conceited,
and no man remembers his Colledge more
at large. The pace of his Sermon is a fall
careere, and he runnes wildly over hill and
dale : till the clocke stop him. The labour

of it is chiefly in his lungs. And the onely thing hee ha's made in it himselfe, is the faces. He takes on against the Pope without mercy, and ha's a jest still in lavender for Bellarmine. Yet he preaches heresie, if it comes in his way, though with a minde I must needs say, very Orthodoxe, His action is all passion, and his speech interjections: Hee ha's an excellent faculty in bemoaning the people, and spits with a very good grace. His stile is compounded of twenty severall mens, onely his body imitates some one extraordinary. He will not draw his handkercher out of his place, nor blow his nose without discretion. His commendation is, that he never looks upon booke, & indeed, hee was never vs'd to it. Hee preaches but once a yeere, though twice a Sunday: for the stuffe is still the same, onely the dressing a little alter'd, He ha's more tricks with a Sermon, then a Tailor with an old cloake to turne it, and piece it, and at last quite disguise it with a new preface. If he have waded further in his profession, and would shew reading of his own, his Authors are Postils, and his Schoole-divinity a Catechisme. His fashion & demure Habit gets him in with some Towne-precisian, & makes him a Guest on Friday nights. You shall

4

know him by his narrow Velvet cape, and
Serge facing, and his ruffe, next his hire;
the shortest thing about him. The companion of his walke is some zealous tradesman
whom he astonisheth with strange points,
which they both vnderstand alike. His
friends and much painefulnesse may pre-
ferre him to thirtie pounds a yeere, and this
meanes, to a Chamber-maide: with whom wee
leaue him now in the bonds of Wedlocke.
Next Sunday you shall haue him againe.

3.   A GRAVE DIVINE

IS one that knowes the burden of his calling, & hath studied to make his shoulders
sufficient: for which hee hath not beene hasty
to launch forth of his port the Vniversitie,
but expected the ballast of learning, and the
winde of opportunity. Divinity is not the
beginning, but the end of his studies, to
which hee takes the ordinary stayre, and
makes the Arts his way. He counts it not
prophanesse to bee polisht with humane
reading, or to smooth his way by Aristotle
to Schoole-Divinity. He ha's founded both
Religions, and anchord in the best, and is
a Protestant out of judgement, not faction,
not because his Country, but his reason is

on this side. The ministry is his choyce, not refuge, and yet the Pulpit not his itch, but feare. His discourse there is substance, not all Rethorique, & he utters more things then words. His speech is not help'd with inforc'd action, but the matter acts it selfe. Hee shoots all his meditations at one But: and beats upon his Text, not the Cushion, making his hearers, not the Pulpit groane. In citing of Popish errors, he cuts them with Arguments, not cudgels them with barren invectives : and labours more to shew the truth of his cause then the spleene. His Sermon is limited by the method, not the houre-glasse ; and his Devotion goes along with him out of the Pulpit. Hee comes not vp thrice a weeke, because he would not bee idle, nor talkes three houres together, because hee would not talke nothing : but his tongue preaches at fit times, and his conuersation is the every dayes exercise. In matters of ceremonie he is not ceremonious, but thinkes hee owes that reverence to the Church to bow his judgement to it, and make more conscience of schisme, then a Surplesse. Hee esteemes the Churches Hierachy as the Churches glory, and how-ever we jarre with Rome, would not have our confusion distinguish vs. In Symoniacall

6

purchases he thinkes his Soule goes in the bargaine, and is loth to come by promotion so deare. Yet his worth at the length aduances him, and the price of his owne merit buies him a living. He is no base grater of his Tythes, and will not wrangle for the odde Egge. The Lawier is the onely man he hinders, by whom he is spited for taking up quarrels. He is a maine pillar of our Church, though not yet Deane nor Canon, and his life our Religions best Apologie. His death is the last Sermon, where in the Pulpit of his Bed, he instructs men to die by his example.

4.   A MODEST MAN.

IS a far finer man then he knowes of, One that shewes better to all men then himselfe, and so much the better to al men, as lesse to himselfe : for no quality sets a man off like this, and commends him more against his will : And he can put up any injury sooner then this (as he cals it) your Irony. You shall heare him confute his commenders, and giving reasons how much they are mistaken, and is angry almost if they doe not beleeve him. Nothing threatens him so much as great expectation, which he thinks

7

more prejudiciall, then your under-opinion, because it is easier to make that false; then this true. He is one that speaks from a good action, as one that had pilfered, and dare not justifie it, and is more blushingly reprehended in this, then others in sin. That counts al publike declarings of himselfe, but so many penances before the people, and the more you applaud him, the more you abash him, and he recovers not his face a moneth after. One that is easie to like any thing, of another mans: and thinkes all he knowes not of him better, then that he knowes. He excuses that to you, which another would impute, and if you pardon him, is satisfied. One that stands in no opinion because it is his owne, but suspects it rather, because it is his owne, and is confuted and thankes you. Hee sees nothing more willingly then his errors; and it is his error sometimes to be too soone perswaded. He is content to be Auditor, where hee only can speake, and content to goe away, and thinke himselfe instructed. No man is so weake that he is ashamed to learne of, and is lesse ashamed to confesse it : and he findes many times even in the dust, what others overlooke, and lose. Every mans presence is a kinde of bridle to him, to stop the roving of his tongue and passions : and even impudent men looke for this reverence from him, and distaste that in him, which they suffer in themselves, as one in whom vice is ill-favoured, & shewes more securvily then another. A bawdy jest shall shame him more then a bastard another man, & he that got it, shall censure him among the rest. And hee is coward to nothing more then an ill tongue, and whosoever dare lye on him hath power over him, & if you take him by his looke, he is guilty. The maine ambition of his life is not to be discredited : and for other things, his desires are more limited then his fortunes, which he thinkes preferment though never so meane, and that he is to doe something to deserve this : Hee is too tender to venter on great places, and would not hurt a dignity to helpe himselfe. If he doe, it was the violence of his friends constrained him, and how hardly soever hee obtaine it, he was harder perswaded to seeke it.

5.   A MEERE DULL PHYSICIAN

HIS practice is some businesse at Bedsides, & his speculation an Vrinall. He is distinguisht from an Empericke, by a round velvet cap, and Doctors gowne, yet no man takes degrees more superfluously, for he is a Doctor how soever. Hee is sworne to Galen and Hypocrates, as Vniversity men to their statutes, though they never saw them, and his discourse is all Aphorismes, though his reading be onely Alexis of piemont, or the Regiment of Health. The best Cure hee ha's done, is upon his own purse, which from a leane sickelinesse he hath made lusty, and in flesh. His learning consists much in reckoning up the hard names of diseases, and the superscriptions of Gally-Pots in his Apothecaries Shoppe, which was rank't in his Shelves : and the Doctors memory. Hee is indeed onely languag'd in diseases, and speakes Greeke many times when he knows not. If he have beene but a by-stander at some desperate recovery, hee is slandered with it, though he be guiltlesse ; and this breeds his reputation, & that his Practice ; for his skill is meerly opinion. Of all odors he likes best the smell of Vrine, and holds Vespasians rule, that no gaine is unsavory. If you send this once to him, you must resolve to be sicke howsoever, for he will never leave examining your Water, till he have shakt it into a disease. Then followes a writ to his Drugger in a strange tongue, which hee understands, though he cannot

conster.   If he see you himselfe, his presence
is the worst visitation: for if hee cannot heale
your sicknesse, he will bee sure to helpe it.
He translates his Apothecaries Shop into
your Chamber and the very Windowes and
benches must take Physicke.   He tells you
your maladie in Greeke, though it be but a
cold, or head-ach: which by good endeavour
and diligence he may bring to some moment
indeed: His most unfaithfull act is, that hee
leaves a man gasping, and his pretence is
death, and he have a quarrell and must not
meete; but his feare is, lest the Carkasse
should bleed.   Anatomies & other spectacles
of Mortalitie have hardned him, and hee's
no more struck with a Funerall then a Graue-
maker.   Noble men vse him for a director
of their stomacks, and Ladies for wanton-
nesse, especially if hee bee a proper man, if
hee be single, hee is in league with his Shee-
Apothecary, and because it is the Physician,
the husband is patient.   If hee have leasure
to be idle (that is to study) hee ha's a snatch
at Alcumy, and is sicke of the Philosophers
stone, a disease uncurable, but by an abun-
dant Phlebotomy of the purse.   His two
maine opposites are a Mountebanke and
a good Woman, and hee never shewes his
learning so much as in an invective against

them & their boxes. In conclusion he is a sucking consumption himself, and a very brother to the Wormes, for they are both ingendred out of mans corruption.

6. A MEERE EMPTY WIT.

IS like one that spends on the stocke without any revenues comming in, and will shortly be no wit at al, for learning is the fuell to the fire of wit, which if it wants this feeding, eates out it selfe. A good conceit or two bates of such a man & makes a sensible weakning in him: and his braine recovers it not a yeere after. The rest of him are bubbles and flashes, darted out on the sudden, which if you take them while they are warme, may be laught at ; if they coole, are nothing. He speakes best on the present apprehension, for Meditation stupifies him, and the more he is in travell, the lesse he brings forth. His things come off then, as in a nauseating stomacke, where there is nothing to cast up straines, & convulsions, and some astonishing bumbast which men onely, till they understand, are scar'd with. A verse or some such worke he may sometimes get up to, but seldome above the stature of an Epigram, and that with some reliefe out of Martial, which is the ordinary companion of his pocket, & he reades him as he were inspir'd. Such men are commonly the trifling things of the World, good to make merry the company, and whom only men have to doe withall, when they have nothing to doe, and none are lesse their friends, then who are most their company. Here they vent themselves o're a cup some-what more lastingly, all their words goe for jests, and all their jests for nothing. They are nimble in the fancy of some ridiculous thing, and reasonable good in the expression. Nothing stops a jest when its comming, neither friends, nor danger, but it must out howsoever, though their blood come out after, and then they emphatically raile and are emphatically beaten, and commonly are men reasonable familiar to this. Briefely they are such whose life is but to laugh, and be laught at: and onely wits in jest, and fooles in earnest.

7.   A MEERE ALDERMAN.

HE is Venerable in his Gowne, more in his Beard, wherewith hee sets not forth so much his owne, as the face of a City. You must looke on him as one of the Towne Gates, and consider him not as a Body, but a Corporation. His eminency above others hath made him a man of Worship, for hee had never beene prefer'd, but that hee was worth thousands. Hee over-sees the Common-wealth, as his Shop, and it is an argument of his policy, that he ha's thriven by his craft. Hee is a rigorous Magistrate in his Ward: yet his scale of justice is suspected, lest it bee like the Ballances in his Warehouse. A ponderous man he is, and substantiall: for his weight is commonly extraordinary, and in his preferment nothing rises so much as his Belly. His head is of no great depth, yet well furnish't, and when it is in conjunction with his Brethren, may bring forth a City Apophthegme, or some such sage matter. He is one that will not hastily runne into error, for hee treades with great deliberation, and his judgement consists much in his pace. His discourse is commonly the Annals of his Majoralty, and what good government there was in the dayes of his gold Chaine: though his doore-posts were the onely things that suffered reforma-tion: Hee seemes most sincerely religious, especially on solemne daies, for he comes oft to Church to make a shew, and is a part of the Quire-hangings. Hee is the highest stair of his profession, and an example to his

Trade, what in time they may come to. He makes very much of his authority: but more of his sattin doublet; which though of good yeeres, beares its age very wel, and lookes fresh every Sunday; But his Scarlet gowne is a Monument, and lasts from generation to generation.

8.   A DISCONTENTED MAN.

IS one that is falne out with the world, & will bee revenged on himselfe. Fortune ha's deny'd him in something, & hee now takes pet, and will bee miserable in spite. The roote of his disease is a selfe-humouring pride, and an accustomed tendernesse, not to bee crost in his fancy: and the occasion's commonly one of these three: a hard Father, a peevish Wench, or his ambition thwarted. Hee considered not the nature of the world till he felt it, and all blowes fall on him heavier, because they light not first on his expectation. Hee ha's now forgone all but his pride, and is yet vaine-glorious in the ostentation of his melancholy. His composure of himself is a studied carelesnesse with his armes a-crosse, and a neglected hanging of his head and cloake, and hee is as great an enemy to an hat-band, as Fortune.

He quarrels at the time, and up-starts, and sighs at the neglect of men of Parts, that is, such as himselfe. His life is a perpetuall Satyre, and hee is still girding the ages vanity; when this very anger shewes he too much esteemes it. Hee is much displeas'd to see men merry, and wonders what they can finde to laugh at. Hee never drawes his owne lips higher then a smile, & frownes wrinkle him before forty. Hee at the last fals into that deadly melancholy to bee a bitter hater of men, and is the most apt Companion for any mischiefe. Hee is the sparke that kindles the Commonwealth, and the bellowes himselfe to blow it: and if hee turne any thing, it is commonly one of these, either Frier, Traytor, or Mad-man.

9. AN ANTIQUARY.

HEE is a man strangely thrifty of Time past, and an enemy indeed to his Maw, whence he fetches out many things when they are now all rotten & stinking. Hee is one that hath that unnaturall disease to bee enamour'd of old age and wrinckles, and loves all things (as Dutchmen doe Cheese) the better for being mouldy and worme-eaten. He is of our Religion, because wee

say it is most ancient; and yet a broken
Statue would almost make him an Idolater.
A great admirer hee is of the rust of old
Monuments, and reades onely those Char-
acters, where time hath eaten out the letters.
Hee will goe you forty miles to see a Saints
Well, or a ruin'd Abbey, and if there be
but a Crosse or stone footstoole in the way,
hee'l be considering it so long, till he forget
his journey. His estate consists much in
shekels, & Roman Coynes, & he hath more
pictures of Cæsar, then Iames, or Elizabeth:
Beggers coozen him with musty things which
they have rak't from dunghills, and he
preserves their rags for precious Reliques.
He loves no Library, but where there are more
Spiders volums then Authors, and lookes
with great admiration on the Antique worke
of Cob-webs. Printed bookes he contemnes,
as a novelty of this latter age, but a Manu-
script hee pores on everlastingly, especially
if the cover be all Moth-eaten, and the dust
make a Parenthesis betweene every Syllable.
He would give all the Bookes in his study
(which are rarities all) for one of the old
Romane binding, or sixe lines of Tully, in his
owne hand. His chamber is hung commonly
with strange Beasts skins, and is a kinde
of Charnel-house of bones extraordinary,

and his discourse upon them, if you will heare him, shall last longer. His very attyre is that which is the eldest out of fashion, and you may picke a Criticisme out of his Breeches. He never lookes up on himself til he is gray-hair'd, and then he is pleased with his owne Antiquity. His Grave do's not fright him, for he ha's bene us'd to Sepulchers, and he likes Death the better, because it gathers him to his Fathers.

10. A DRUNKARD.

IS one that will be a man to morrow morning: but is now what you will make him, for he is in the power of the next man, & if a friend, the better. One that hath let goe himselfe from the hold & stay of reason, and lyes open to the mercy of all temptations. No lust but findes him disarmed and fencelesse, and with the least assault enters. If any mischiefe escape him, it was not his fault, for he was layd as faire for it, as he could. Every man sees him, as Cham saw his Father the first of this sinne, an uncover'd man, and, though his garment be on, uncover'd, the secretest parts of his soule lying in the nakedst manner visible: all his passions come out now, all his vanities, &

those shamefuller humors which discretion clothes. His body becomes at last like a myrie way, where the spirits are be clog'd and cannot passe: all his members are out of office, and his heeles doe but trip up one another. He is a blind man with eyes, and a Cripple with legs on. All the use he ha's of this vessell himselfe, is to hold thus much: for his drinking is but a scooping in of so many quarts, which are filld out into his body, and that fild out again into the Roome, which is commonly as drunke as hee. Tobacco serves to aire him after a washing, and is his onely breath, and breathing while. Hee is the greatest enemy to himselfe, and the next to his friend, and then most in the act of his kindnesse, for his kindnesse is but trying a mastery, who shall sinke down first: And men come from him as a battel, wounded, and bound up. Nothing takes a man off more from his credit, and businesse, and makes him more retchlesly carelesse, what becomes of all. Indeed hee dares not enter on a serious thought, or if hee doe, it is such melancholy, that it sends him to be drunke againe.

11.   YOUNGER BROTHER.

HIS elder Brother was the Esau, that came
out first and left him like Iacob at his heeles.
His Father ha's done with him, as Pharaoh
to the Children of Israel, that would have
them make bricke, and give them no straw,
so he taskes him to bee a Gentleman, and
leaves him nothing to maintaine it.   The
pride of his house ha's undone him, which
the elders Knighthood must sustaine, and
his beggery that Knighthood.   His birth
and bringing up, will not suffer him to
descend to the meanes to get wealth : but he
stands at the mercy of the World, and, which
is worse, of his brother.   He is something
better then the Servingmen : yet they more
saucy with him, then hee bold with the
master, who beholds him with a countenance of sterne awe, and checks him oftner
then his Liveries.   His brothers old suites
and he are much alike in request, and cast
off now and then one to the other.   Nature
hath furnisht him with a little more wit
upon compassion ; for it is like to be his
best revenue.   If his Annuity stretch so farre,
he is sent to the Vniversity, and with great
heart-burning takes upon him the Ministry,
as a profession hee is condemn'd to : by his

ill fortune others take a more croked path, yet the Kings high-way; where at length their vizzard is pluck't off, and they strike faire for Tiborne : but their Brothers pride, not love gets them a pardon. His last refuge is the Low-countries, where rags and lice are no scandall, where he lives a poore Gentleman of a Company, & dies without a shirt. The onely thing that may better his fortunes, is an art he ha's to make a Gentlewoman, wherewith hee baits now and then some rich widow, that is hungry after his Blood. Hee is commonly discontented and desperate, & the forme of his exclamation is, that Churle my Brother. He loves not his Country for this unnaturall custom, & would have long since revolted to the Spaniard, but for Kent onely which he holds in admiration.

12. A MEERE FORMALL MAN.

IS somewhat more then the shape of a man; for he ha's his length, breadth, and colour. When you have seene his outside, you have lookt thorow him, & need imploy your discovery no farther. His reason is meerly example; and his action is not guided by his understanding, but hee sees other men doe thus, and he followes them. He is a

Negative, for wee cannot call him a wise man, but not a foole; nor an honest man, but not a knave; nor a Protestant, but not a Papist. The chiefe burden of his braine is the carriage of his body and the setting of his face in a good frame: which hee performes the better, because hee is not disjoynted with other Meditations. His Religion is a good quiet subject, & he prayes as he sweares, in the Phrase of the Land. He is a faire guest, and a faire inviter, and can excuse his good cheere in the accustomed Apologie. He ha's some faculty in mangling of a Rabbet, and the distribution of his morsell to a neighbour trencher. Hee apprehends a jest by seeing men smile, and laughs orderly himselfe, when it comes to his turne. His businesses with his friends are to visit them, and whilst the businesse is no more, he can performe this well enough. His discourse is the newes that he hath gathered in his walke, & for other matters his discretion is, that hee will onely what hee can, that is, say nothing. His life is like one that runnes to the Church-walke, to take a turne, or two, and so passes. He hath staid in the world to fill a number; and when he is gone, there wants one, and there's an end.

13. A CHURCH-PAPIST

IS one that parts his Religion betwixt his conscience & his purse, & comes to Church not to serve God, but the King. The face of the Law makes him weare the maske of the Gospell, which he uses not as a meanes to save his soule, but charges. He loues Popery well, but is loth to lose by it, and though he be something scar'd with the Buls of Rome, yet they are farre off, and he is strucke with more terrour at the Apparitor. Once a moneth he presents himselfe at the Church, to keepe off the Church-warden, and brings in his body to save his bayle. He kneeles with the Congregation, but prayes by himselfe, and askes God forgivenesse for comming thither. If he be forced to stay out a Sermon, he puls his hat over his eyes, and frownes out the houre, and when hee comes home, thinkes to make amends for this fault by abusing the Preacher. His maine policy is to shift off the Communion, for which he is never unfurnish't of a quarrell, & will be sure to be out of Charity at Easter; and indeed he lies not, for hee ha's a quarrell to the Sacrament. He would make a bad Martyr, and good traveller, for his conscience is so large, he could never wander out of it, and in Constantinople would be circumcis'd with a reservation. His wife is more zealous, and therefore more costly, and he bates her in tyres what she stands him in Religion. But we leave him hatching plots against the State, and expecting Spinola.

14. A PRISON

IS the grave of the living, where they are shut up from the world, and their friends : and the wormes that gnaw upon them, their owne thoughts, and the Iaylor.   A house of meager lookes, and ill smells : for lice, drink, Tobacco, are the compound ; Pluto's Court was express't from this fancy.   And the persons are much about the same parity that is there. You may aske as Manippus in Lucian, which is Nireus, which Thersites which the begger, which the Knight : for they are all suited in the same forme of a kinde of nasty poverty.   Onely to be out at elbowes is in fashion here, and a great Indecorum, not to be thred-bare. Every man shewes here like so many wrackes upon the Sea, here the ribs of a thousand pound, here the relicke of so many Mannours, a doublet without buttons.

And tis a spectacle of more pitty then executions are.   The company one with other, is
but a vieing of complaints, and the causes
they have, to rayle on fortune, the foole
themselves, and there is a great deale of
good-fellowship in this. They are commonly,
next their Creditors, most bitter against the
Lawyers, as men that have had a great stroke
in assisting them hither.   Mirth here is
stupidity or hardheartednes, yet they faine
it sometimes to slip melancholy and keepe
off themselves from themselves, and the
torment of thinking what they have beene.
Men huddle up their Life here as a thing of
no use, and weare it out like an old suite,
the faster the better : and hee that deceives
the time best, best spends it.   It is the place
where new commers are most welcom'd, and
next them ill newes, as that which extends
their fellowship in misery, and leaves fewe
to insult : And they breathe their discontents
more securely here, and have their tongues
at more liberty then abroad.   Men see here
much sin, and much calamity : and where
the last does not mortifie, the other hardens,
and those that are worse here, are desperately worse, as those from whom the horror
of sinne is taken off, and the punishment
familiar.   And commonly a hard thought

25

passes on all, that come from this Schoole: which though it teach much wifedome, it is too late, and with danger: and it is better bee a foole, then come here to learne it.

15.   A SELFE-CONCEITED MAN

IS one that knowes himselfe so wel, that he does not know himselfe.   Two excellent well dones have undone him; and he is guilty of it, that first commended him to madnesse. Hee is now become his owne Booke, which he poares on continually, yet like a truant-reader skips over the harsh places, and surveyes onely that which is pleasant.   In the speculation of his owne good parts, his eyes, like a drunkards, see all double, and his fancy like an old mans Spectacles, make a great letter in a small print.   He imagines every place, where hee comes, his Theater, and not a looke stirring, but his spectator; and conceives mens thoughts to bee very idle, that is, onely busie about him.   His walke is still in the fashion of a March, and, like his opinion, unaccompanied, with his eyes most fixt upon his owne person, or on others with reflection to himselfe.   If he have done any thing that ha's past with applause, hee is always re-acting it alone, & conceits the extasie his hearers were in at every period. His discourse is all positions, and definitive decrees, with thus it must bee, and thus it is, and hee will not humble his authority to prove it. His Tenent is alwayes singular, and a-loofe from the vulgar as he can, from which you must not hope to wrest him, Hee ha's an excellent humour for an Heretique, and in these dayes made the first Arminian. He prefers Ramus before Aristotle and Paracelsus before Galen, & whosoever with most Paradox is commended. He much pitties the world, that ha's no more insight in his parts, when he is too well discovered, even to this very thought. A flatterer is a dunce to him, for he can tell him nothing but what hee knowes before : and yet hee loves him to, because he is like himselfe. Men are mercifull to him : and let him alone, for if he bee once driven from his humour, he is like two inward friends fallen out ; His owne bitter enemy, and discontent presently makes a murther. In summe, he is a bladder blown up with winde, which the least flaw crushes to nothing.

16. A SERVINGMAN.

IS one of the makings up of a Gentleman,
as well as his clothes: and somewhat in the
same nature, for hee is cast behind his
master as fashionably as his sword & cloake
are, and he is but in querpo without him.
His propernesse qualifies him, and of that
a good legge: for his head he ha's little
use but to keep it bare. A good dull wit
best suits with him, to comprehend common
sense, and a trencher: for any greater store
of braine it makes him but tumultuous, and
seldome thrives with him. He followes his
Masters steps, as well in Conditions as the
street: if he wench or drinke he comes after
in an underkind, and thinks it a part of his
duty to be like him. He is indeed wholly
his Masters, of his faction, of his cut, of his
pleasures: he is handsome for his credit, and
drunke for his credit; and if hee have power
in the seller, commands the parish. Hee is
one that keepes the best company, and is
none of it: for he knowes all the Gentlemen
his Master knowes, and pickes from them
some Hawking, and Horse-race termes, which
he swaggers with in the Ale-house, where he
is onely called Master. His mirth is bawdy

jests with the Wenches, and behind the doore bawdy earnest. The best worke he does is his marrying, for it makes an honest woman, and if he follow in it his Masters direction, it is commonly the best service he does him.

17.   A TOO IDLE RESERV'D MAN

IS one that is a foole with discretion : or a strange piece of Politician, that manages the state of himselfe. His Actions are his Privie Counsell, wherein no man must partake beside. He speakes under rule & prescription, and dare not shew his teeth without Machiavell. Hee converses with his neighbours as hee would in Spaine, and feares an inquisitive man as much as the Inquisition. He suspects all questions for examinations, and thinkes you would picke some thing out of him, and avoids you : His brest is like a Gentlewomans closet, which locks up every toye or trifle, or some bragging Mountebanke, that makes every stinking thing a secret. He delivers you common matters with great conjuration of silence, & whispers you in the eare Acts of Parliament. You may as soone wrest a tooth from him as a paper, and whatsoever he reakes is letters. He dares not talke of great men for feare of bad Comments, and hee knowes not how his words may bee misplaced. Aske his opinion and he tels you his doubt: and he never heares any thing more astonishtly then that hee knowes before. His words are like the Cards at Primiviste, where sixe is eighteene, and seven one and twenty, for they never signifie what they sound; but if hee tell you hee will doe a thing, it is as much as if he swore he would not. He is one indeed that takes all men to bee craftier then they are, and puts himselfe to a great deale of affliction to hinder their plots and designes, where they meane freely. He ha's bene long a Riddle himselfe, but at last findes Oedipusses; for his over-acted dissimulation discovers him, and men do with him as they would with Hebrew letters, spell him backwards, and reade him.

18.   A TAVERNE

IS a degree, or (if you will) a paire of staires above an Alehouse, where men are drunke with more credit & Apologie. If the Vintners nose be at doore, it is a signe sufficient, but the absence of this is supplied by the Ivie-bush: The roomes are ill breath'd like the drinkers that have bin washt well

30

over-night, and are smelt too fasting next
morning; not furnisht with beds apt to be
defiled but more necessary implements,
Stooles, Table, and a Chamber-pot. It is a
broacher of more newes then Hogs-heads, and
more jests then newes, which are suckt up
heere by some spungy braine, and from
thence squeaz'd into a Comedy. Men come
heere to make merry, but indeed make a
noise, and this Musicke above is answered
with the clinking below. The Drawers are the
civillest people in it, men of good bringing
up, and howsoever we esteeme of them, none
can boast more justly of their high calling.
'Tis the best Theater of natures, where they
are truly acted, not plaid, and the businesse
as in the rest of the world up and downe,
to wit, from the bottome of the Seller to the
great Chamber. A melancholy Man would
finde here matter to worke upon to see Heads
as brittle as Glasses, and often broken Men
come hither to quarrell, and come hither to
be made friends : and if Plutarch will lend
mee his Simile, it is even Telephus his sword
that makes wounds, and cures them. It is
the common consumption of the Afternoone,
and the murderer, or maker away of a rainy
day. It is the Torrid Zone that scorches
the face, and Tobacco the gun-powder that

blowes it up. Much harme would be done, if the charitable Vintener had not Water ready for these flames. A house of sinne you may call it, but not a house of darkenesse, for the Candles are never out; and it is like those Countries farre in the North, where it is as cleare at mid-night as at mid-day. After a long sitting, it becomes like a street in a dashing showre, where the spouts are flushing above, and the Conduits running below, while the Iordans like swelling rivers overflow their bankes. To give you the totall reckoning of it. It is the busie mans recreation, the idle mans businesse, the melancholy mans Sanctuary, the strangers welcome, the Inns a Court mans entertainment, the Schollers kindnesse, and the Citizens courtesie. It is the study of sparkling wits, and a cup of Sherrey their booke, where we leave them.

19. A SHARKE

IS one whom all other meanes have fail'd, and hee now lives of himselfe. He is some needy cashir'd fellow, whom the World ha's oft flung off, yet still claspes againe, and is like one a drowning, fastens upon any thing that's next at hand. Amongst other of his

Shipwrackes hee ha's happily lost shame, &
this want supplies him. No man puts his
Braine to more use then he, for his life is
a daily invention, and each meale a new
Stratagem. Hee ha's an excellent memory
for his acquaintance, though there past but
How doe you betwixt them seven yeeres agoe,
it shall suffice for an Imbrace, and that for
money. He offers you a Pottle of Sacke out
of his joy to see you, and in requitall of this
courtesie, you can doe no lesse then pay for
it. He is fumbling with his purse-strings,
as a Schoole-boy with his points, when hee
is going to be Whipt, till the Master weary
with long Stay, forgives him. When the
reckoning is paid, he sayes it must not bee
so, yet is strait pacified, and cryes, What
remedy? His borrowings are like Subsidies,
each man a shilling or two, as he can well
dis-pend, which they lend him, not with the
hope to be repayed, but that he will come
no more. He holds a strange tyranny over
men : for he is their Debtor, and they feare
him as a Creditor. He is proud of any
imployment, though it bee but to carry commendations, which he will be sure to deliver
at eleven of the clocke. They in courtesie
bid him stay, & he in manners cannot deny
them. If he finde but a good looke to assure

his welcom, he becomes their halfe boorder, and haunts the threshhold so long, till he forces good natures to the necessity of a quarrell. Publique invitations hee will not wrong with his absence, and is the best witnesse of the Sherifes Hospitality. Men shun him at length as they would doe an infection, and he is never crost in his way, if there be but a lane to escape him. He ha's done with the Age as his clothes to him, hung on as long as hee could, and at last drops off.

20. AN INSOLENT MAN

IS a fellow newly great and newly proud : one that ha's put himselfe into another face upon his preferment, for his owne was not bred to it. One whom Fortune hath shot up to some Office or Authority, and he shoots up his necke to his fortune, and will not bate you an inch of either. His very countenance and gesture bespeak how much he is, and if you understand him not, he tells you, & concludes every Period with his place, which you must and shall know. He is one that lookes on all men as if he were very angry, but especially on those of his acquaintance, whom hee beats off with a surlier distance, as men apt to mistake him, because they

34

have knowne him. And for this cause hee knowes not you till you have told him your name, which hee thinkes hee ha's heard, but forgot, and with much adoe seemes to recover. If you have any thing to use him in, you are his vassall for that time, & must give him the patience of any injury, which hee does only to shew what he may doe. He snaps you up bitterly, because he will be offended, and tels you, you are sawcy and troublesome, and sometimes takes your money in this language. His very Courtesies are intolerable, they are done with such arrogance & imputation, & he is the onely man you may hate after a good turne, and not bee ungratefull, & men reckon it among their calamities to be beholden unto him. No vice drawes with it a more general hostility, & makes men readier to search into his faults, & of them, his beginning : And no tale so unlikely but is willingly heard of him, and beleev'd. And commonly such men are of no merit at all : but make out in pride what they want in worth, and fence themselves with a stately kinde of behaviour from that contempt would pursue them. They are men whose preferment does us a great deale of wrong, & when they are downe, wee may laugh at them, without breach of good Nature.

21. ACQUAINTANCE

IS the first draught of a friend, whom wee must lay downe oft thus, as the soule coppy before we can write him perfit, & true: for from hence, as from a probation, men take a degree in our respect, till at last they wholy possesse us. For acquaintance is the hoard, and friendship the paire chosen out of it: by which at last wee begin to impropriate, and enclose to our selves, what before lay in common with others. And commonly where it growes not up to this, it falls as low as may be: and no poorer relation, then old acquaintance, of whom we aske onely how they doe for fashion sake, & care not. The ordinary use of acquaintance is but somewhat a more boldnesse of society, a sharing of talke, newes, drinke, mirth, together: but sorrow is the right of a friend, as a thing nearer our heart, and to be deliver'd with it. Nothing easier then to create Acquaintance: the meere being in company once, doe's it; whereas friendship like children is ingendred by a more inward mixture, and coupling together: when we are acquainted not with their vertues onely, but their faults to their passions, their feares, their shame, & are bold on both sides to make their discovery. And as it is in the love of the body, which is then at the height and full when it ha's power and admittance into the hidden and worst parts of it : So it is in friendship with the mind, when those verenda of the soule, & those things which wee dare not shew the world, are bare and detected one to another. Some men are familiar with all, and those commonly friends to none : for friendship is a sullener thing, as a Contractor & taker up of our affections to some few, and suffers them not loosly to be scatter'd on all men. The poorest tye of acquaintance is that of place and Country which are shifted as the place, and mist but while the fancy of that continues. These are onely then gladdest of other, when they meet in some forraign region, where the encompassing of strangers unites them closer, till at last they get new, and throw off one another. Men of parts and eminency, as their acquaintance is more sought for, so they are generally more staunch of it, not out of pride onely, but feare to let too many in too neer them, for it is with men as with pictures, the best show better afar off & at distance ; and the closer you come to them, the courser they are. The best judgement of a man, is taken from his Acquaintance : for friends and enemies are both partiall : whereas these see him truest, because calmeliest, and are no way so engag'd to lye for him. And men that grow strange after acquaintance, seldome peece together againe, as those that have tasted meat & dislike it, out of a mutuall experience dis-rellishing one another.

22. A CARRIER

IS his own Hackney man : for he lets himselfe out to travell as well as his horses. Hee is the ordinary Embassadour betweene Friend & Friend, the Father & the Sonne, and brings rich Presents to the one, but never returnes any backe againe. He is no unletter'd man, though in shew simple, for questionlesse, hee ha's much in his Budget, which hee can utter too in fit time & place ; He is like the Vault in Gloster Church ; that conveyes Whispers at a distance ; for hee takes the sound out of your mouth at Yorke ; and makes it be heard as farre as London. He is the young Students joy & expectation, and the most accepted Guest, to whom they lend a willing hand to discharge him of his burthen. His first greeting is commonly, Your Friends are well ; And to prove it, in a piece of Gold delivers their Blessing. You would thinke him a Churlish blunt fellow, but they finde in him many tokens of humanity. He is a great afflicter of the High-way, and beates them out of measure; which injury is sometimes revenged by the Purse taker; and then the Voyage miscarries. No man domineeres more in his Inne, nor calls his Host unreverently with more presumption, & his arrogance proceeds out of the strength of his Horses. He forgets not his load where hee takes his ease: for he is drunke commonly before he goes to bed. He is like the Prodigall Child, still packing away, & still returning againe. But let him passe.

23. A MEERE COMPLEMENTALL MAN

IS one to be held off still at the same distance you are now; for you shall have him but thus, & if you enter on him further, you lose him. Me thinkes Virgil well expresses him in those well-behav'd ghosts that Æneas mette with, that were friends to talke with, and men to looke on, but if he graspt them, but ayre. He is one that lyes kindly to you, & for good fashion sake, and 'tis discourtesie in you to beleeve him. His words are but so many fine phrases set together, which serve equally for all men, and are equally to no purpose. Each fresh encounter with a man, puts him to the same part againe, and he goes over to you ; what hee said to him was last with him. Hee kisses your hands as hee kist his before, and is your servant to bee commanded, but you shall entreat of him nothing. His profers are universall & generall with exceptions against all particulars ; hee will do any thing for you : but if you urge him to this, he cannot, or to that, he is engag'd : but he will doe any thing. Promise he accounts but a kind of mannerly words, & in the expectation of your manners, not to exact them : if you doe, he wonders at your ill breeding, that cannot distinguish betwixt what is spoken, and what is meant : No man gives better satisfaction at the first, and comes off more with the Elogie of a kinde Gentleman, till you know him better, and then you know him for nothing. And commonly those most raile at him, that have before most commended him. The best is, he coozens you in a faire manner, and abuses you with great respect.

24.   A POORE FIDLER

IS a Man and a Fiddle out of case : and
he in worse case then his Fiddle.   One that
rubs two stickes together (as the Indians
strike fire) and rubs a poore living out of
it : Partly from this, and partly from your
charity, which is more in the hearing, then
giving him, For he sells nothing dearer then
to be gone : He is just so many strings above
a begger, though he have but two : and yet
he begs too, onely not in the downe-right for
Gods sake, but with a shrugging God blesse
you, & his face is more pin'd then the blind
mans.   Hunger is the greatest paine he takes,
except a broken head sometimes, and the
labouring Iohn Dorry.   Otherwise his life
is so many fits of mirth, and 'tis some mirth
to see him.   A good feast shall draw him
five miles by the nose, & you shall tracke him
againe by the sent.   His other Pilgrimages
are Faires, and good Houses, where his
devotion is great to the Christmas : and no
man loves good times better.   He is in league
with the Tapsters for the worshipfull of the
Inne, whom hee torments next morning with
his art, & ha's their Names more perfit then
their men.   A new song is better to him

then a new Iacket : especially if bawdy, which
he calls merry, & hates naturally the Puritan,
as an enemy to this mirth. A Country
Wedding, and Whitson-ale are the two maine
places he dominiers in, where he goes for a
Musician, & over-lookes the Bag-pipe. The
rest of him is drunke, and in the Stocks.

25. A YOUNG MAN.

HEE is now out of Natures protection,
though not yet able to guide himselfe : But left
loose to the World, and Fortune from which
the weaknesse of his Childhood preseru'd
him : And now his strength exposes him.
He is indeed just of age to be miserable,
yet in his owne conceit first beginnes to be
happy ; and he is happier in this imagina-
tion, and his misery not felt is lesse. He
sees yet but the outside of the World and
Men, and conceives them according to their
appearing glister, and out of this ignorance
beleeves them. He pursues all vanities for
happinesse, and enjoyes them best in this
fancy. His reason serves not to curbe, but
understand his appetite, and prosecute the
motions thereof with a more eager earnestnes.
Himselfe is his owne temptation, and needs
not Satan, and the World will come hereafter.

He leaves repentance for gray haires, and performes it in being covetous. He is mingled with the vices of the age as the fashion and custome, with which he longs to bee acquainted ; & Sinnes, to better his understanding. He conceives his Youth as the season of his Lust, and the houre wherein hee ought to be bad : and because he would not lose his time, spends it. He distasts Religion as a sad thing, and is sixe yeeres elder for a thought of Heaven. Hee scornes and feares, and yet hopes for old age, but dare not imagine it with wrinkles. Hee loves and hates with the same inflamation : and when the heat is over is coole alike to friends & enemies. His friendship is seldom so stedfast, but that lust, drinke, or anger may overturne it. He offers you his blood to day in kindnesse, and is ready to take yours to morrow. He do's seldome any thing which hee wishes not to doe againe, and is onely wise after a misfortune. Hee suffers much for his knowledge, and a great deale of folly it is makes him a wise man. He is free from many Vices, by being not grown to the performance, & is onely more vertuous out of weakenesse. Every action is his danger, & every man his ambush. Hee is a Shippe without Pilot or Tackling, and onely good fortune may steere him. If he scape this age, hee ha's scap't a Tempest, & may live to be a Man.

26. AN OLD COLLEDGE BUTLER

IS none of the worst Students in the house, for he keepes the set houres at his book more duly then any. His authority is great over mens good names, which hee charges many times with shrewd aspersions, which they hardly wipe off without payment. His Boxe and Counters prove him to be a man of reckoning; yet hee is stricter in his accounts then a Vsurer, and delivers not a farthing without writing. He doubles the paines of Gallobelgicus, for his Bookes goe out once a quarter, & they are much in the same nature, briefe notes and Summes of affaires, and are out of request as soone. His commings in are like a Taylors from the shreds of bread, the chippings, and remnants of the broken crust : excepting his vailes from the barrell, which poore folkes buy for their Hogs, but drinke themselves. He divides a halfepenny loafe with more subtilty then Kekerman, & sub-divides the A primo ortum so nicely, that a stomacke of great capacity can hardly apprehend it. Hee is a very sober man, considering his manifold temptations of drinke and strangers, & if he be over-seene, 'tis within his owne liberties, and no man ought to take exception. He is never so well pleas'd with his place, as when a Gentleman is beholding to him for shewing him the Buttery, whom hee greets with a cup of single Beere, and slyst Manchet, and tels him 'Tis the fashion of the Colledge. Hee domineers over Freshmen when they first come to the Hatch, and puzzles them with strange language of Cues, and Cees, and some broken Latine which he ha's learnt at his Bin. His faculties extraordinary, is the warming of a paire of Cards, and telling out a doozen of Counters for Post and Paire, and no man is more methodicall in these businesses. Thus hee spends his age, till the tappe of it is runne out, and then a fresh one is set abroach.

27.   A MEDLING MAN

IS one that ha's nothing to do with his businesse, and yet no man busier then hee, and his businesse is most in his face. He is one thrusts himselfe violently into all imployments, unsent for, un-feed, and many times un-thank't, & his part in it is onely an eager bustling, that rather keepes adoe, then

45

do's any thing. He will take you aside, and
question you of your affaire, and listen with
both eares, and looke earnestly : and then
it is nothing so much yours as his. Hee
snatches what you are doing out of your
hands, and cryes Give it mee, and does it
worse, and layes an engagement upon you
too, & you must thanke him for this paines.
Hee layes you down a hundred wild plots,
all impossible things, which you must bee
ruled by perforce, and hee delivers them
with a serious and counselling forehead, &
there is a great deale more wisedome in this
forehead, then his head : He will woo for you,
sollicite for you, and woo you to suffer him :
& scarce any thing done, wherein his letter,
or his journey, or at least himselfe is not
seene, if he have no taske in it else, he will
raile yet on some side, and is often beaten
when hee need not. Such men never thorowly
weigh any businesse, but are forward onely
to shew their zeale, when many times this
forwardnesse spoiles it, and then they cry
they have done what they can, that is as
much hurt. Wise men still deprecate these
mens kindnesses, & are beholding to them
rather to let them alone ; as being one trouble
more in all businesse, & which a man shall
be hardest rid of.

28. AN VPSTART KNIGHT

IS a Holi-day Clowne, & differs onely in
the stuffe of his Clothes, not the stuffe of
himselfe: for hee bare the Kings sword before
he had armes to wield it; yet being once
laid o're the shoulder with a Knighthood,
he finds the Herauld his friend. His father
was a man of good stocke, though but a
Tanner, or Vsurer; hee purchast the Land,
and his son the Title. He ha's doft off the
name of a Country fellow, but the looke not
so easie, and his face beares still a relish of
Churne-milke. He is garded with more Gold
lace then all the Gentlemen o'th Country,
yet his body makes his clothes stil out of
fashion. His house-keeping is seene much
in the distinct families of Dogs, & Servingmen attendant on their kennels, and the
deepnesse of their throats is the depth of
their discourse. A Hawke he esteemes the
true burthen of Nobility, and is exceeding
ambitious to seeme delighted in the sport,
and have his fist Glov'd with his Iesses. A
Iustice of peace hee is to domineere in his
Parish, and doe his Neighbour wrong with
more right. Hee will bee drunke with his
Hunters for company, & staine his Gentility

47

with droppings of Ale. He is fearefull of being Sherife of the Shire by instinct; and dreads the Size-weeke as much as the prisoner. In summe, he's but a clod of his owne earth; or his Land is the Dunghill, and he the Cocke that crowes over it. And commonly his race is quickely runne, and his Childrens Children, though they scape hanging, returne to the place from whence they came.

29. A GOOD OLD MAN

IS the best Antiquity, & which we may with least vanity admire. One whom Time hath beene thus long a working, and like Winter fruit ripen'd when others are shaken downe. He hath taken out as many lessons of the world, as dayes, and learn't the best thing in it, the vanity of it. Hee lookes o're his former life as a danger well past, and would not hazard himselfe to begin againe. His lust was long broken before his body, yet he is glad this temptation is broke too, & that he is fortified from it by this weakenesse. The next doore of death sads him not, but hee expects it calmely as his turne in Nature: and feares more his recoyling backe to childishnes then dust. All men looke on him as a common Father, and on old age for his sake, as a reverent thing. His very presence, & face puts vice out of countenance, and makes it an indecorum in a vicious man. Hee practises his experience on youth without the harshnesse of reproofe, and in his counsell his good compeny. Hee ha's some old stories still of his owne seeing to confirme what he sayes, and makes them better in the telling: yet is not troublesome neither with the same tale againe, but remembers with them, how oft he ha's told them. His old sayings & moralls seeme proper to his beard: and the poetry of Cato do's well out of his mouth, and he speakes it, as if hee were the Author. Hee is not apt to put the boy on a yonger man, nor the foole on a Boy, but can distinguish gravity from a sowre looke, and the lesse testy he is, the more regarded. You must pardon him if he like his owne times better then these, because those things are follies to him now that were wisedome then: yet he makes us of that opinion too, when we see him, and conjecture those times by so good a Relicke. He is a man capable of a dearenesse with the youngest men; yet he not youthfuller for them, but they older for him, and no man credits more his acquaintance. He goes away at last too soone whensoever, with all mens sorrow but his owne, and his memory is fresh, when it is twice as old.

30. A GALLANT

IS one that was borne and shapt for his Cloathes: and if Adam had not falne, had liv'd to no purpose: Hee gratulates therefore the first sinne; and fig-leaves that were an occasion of bravery. His first care is his dresse, the next his body, and in the uniting of these two lyes his soule and its faculties. He observes London trulier then the Termes; & his businesse is the street, the Stage, the Court, and those places where a proper man is best showne. If hee be qualified in gaming extraordinary, he is so much the more gentle & compleate, & hee learnes the best oathes for the purpose. These are a great part of his discourse, and he is as curious in their newnesse as the fashion. His other talke is Ladies and such pretty things, or some jest at a Play. His Pick-tooth beares a great part in his discourse, so does his body; the upper parts whereof are as starcht as his linnen, and perchance use the same Laundresse. Hee ha's learnt to ruffle his face from his Boote, and takes a great delight in his walke to heare his Spurs gingle. Though his life passe somewhat slidingly, yet he seemes very carefull of the time, for hee is still drawing his Watch out of his Pocket, and spends part of his houres in numbring them. He is one never serious but with his Taylor, when hee is in conspiracy for the next device. He is furnisht with his Iests, as some wanderer with Sermons, some three for all Congregations, one especially against the Scholler, a man to him much ridiculous, whom hee knowes by no other definition, but silly fellow in blacke. He is a kinde of walking Mercers Shop, and shewes you one Stuffe to day, and another to morrow, an ornament to the roomes he comes in, as the faire Bed and Hangings be ; and is meerely ratable accordingly, fifty or an hundred Pound as his suit is. His maine ambition is to get a Knight-hood, & then an old Lady, which if he be happy in, he fils the Stage and a Coach so much longer. Otherwise, himselfe and his cloaths grow stale together, and he is buried commonly ere he dies in the Gaole, or the Country.

31. A CONSTABLE

IS a Vice-roy in the street & no man stands more upon't that he is the Kings Officer. His Iurisdiction extends to the next stocks, where hee ha's Commission for the heeles onely, & sets the rest of the body at liberty. He is a Scar-crow to that Ale-house, where he drinkes not his mornings draught, and apprehends a Drunkard for not standing in the Kings Name. Beggers feare him more then the Iustice, & as much as the Whipstocke, whom hee delivers over to his subordinate Magistrates, the Bride-wel-man, and the Beadle. Hee is a great stickler in the tumults of double Iugges, and ventures his head by his Place, which is broke many times to keep whole the peace. He is never so much in his majestie, as in his night-watch, where hee sits in his Chayre of State, a Shop-stall, and inviron'd with a guard of Halberts, examines all passengers. He is a very carefull man in his Office, but if hee stay up after Midnight, you shall take him napping.

32. A FLATTERER

IS the picture of a friend, & as pictures
flatter many times, so hee oft shewes fairer
then the true substance : His looke, conversation, company, and all the outwardnesse
of friendship more pleasing by odds, for
a true friend dare take the liberty to bee
sometimes offensive, wheras he is a great
deale more cowardly, & will not let the least
hold goe, for feare of losing you. Your meere
sowre looke affrights him, and makes him
doubt his casheering. And this is one sure
marke of him, that he is never first angry,
but ready, though upon his owne wrong, to
make satisfaction. Therefore hee is never
yok't with a poore man, or any that stands
on the lower ground, but whose fortunes may
tempt his paines to deceive him. Him hee
learnes first, and learnes well, and growes
perfitter in his humours, then himselfe, & by
this doore enters upon his Soule : of which
hee is able at last to take the very print and
marke, and fashion his own by it like a false
key to open all your secrets. All his affections jumpe even with yours : hee is before
hand with your thoughts, & able to suggest
them unto you. He will commend to you

first, what hee knowes you like, & ha's alwayes some absurd story or other of your enemy, and then wonders how your two opinions should jumpe in that man. Hee will aske your counsell sometimes as a man of deepe judgement, and ha's a secret of purpose to disclose you, and whatsoever you say, is perswaded. He listens to your words with great attention, and sometimes wil object that you may confute him, and then protests hee never heard so much before. A piece of witte bursts him with an overflowing laughter, & hee remembers it for you to all companies, and laughs againe in the telling. He is one never chides you but for your vertues, as, You are too good, too honest, too religious ; when his chiding may seeme but the earnester commendation, and yet would faine chide you out of them too : for your vice is the thing he ha's use of, and wherein you may best use him, and hee is never more active then in the worst diligences. Thus at last he possesses you from your selfe, and then expects but his hire to betray you. And it is a happinesse not to discover him ; for as long as you are happy, you shall not.

33. A DOWNE-RIGHT SCHOLLER

IS one that ha's much learning in the Ore, unwrought, and untryde, which time and experience fashions and refines. He is good mettall in the inside, though rough and unscour'd without, & therefore hated of the Courtier, that is quite contrary. The time ha's got a veine of making him ridiculous, and men laugh at him by tradition, and no unlucky absurdity; but is put upon his profession, and done like a Scholler. But his fault is onely this, that his mind is somewhat too much taken up with his minde, and his thoughts not loaden with any carriage besides. He has not put on the quaint Garb of the Age, which is now a mans Imprimis & all the Item. He ha's not humbled his Meditations to the industry of Complement, nor afflicted his braine in an elaborate legge. His body is not set upon nice Pins to be turning and flexible for every motion, but his scrape is homely, and his nod worse, He cannot kisse his hand & cry Madame, nor talke idly enough to beare her company. His smacking of a Gentle-woman is somewhat too savory, and hee mistakes her nose for her lippe. A very

Wodcocke would puzzle him in carving, and hee wants the logicke of a Capon. Hee ha's not the glib faculty of sliding over a tale, but his words come squeamishly out of his mouth, and the laughter commonly before the jest. Hee names this word Colledge too often, and his discourse beats too much on the Vniversity. The perplexity of mannerlinesse will not let him feed, and hee is sharpe set at an argument when hee should cut his meat. He is discarded for a gamester at all games but one & thirty, & at tables hee reaches not beyond Doublets. His fingers are not long and drawn out to handle a Fiddle, but his fist is cluncht with the habite of disputing. He ascends a horse somwhat sinisterly, though not on the left side, and they both goe jogging in griefe together. He is exceedingly censur'd by the Innes a Court men, for that hainous vice beeing out of fashion. He cannot speake to a Dogge in his owne Dialect, & understands Greeke better then the language of a Faulconer. Hee ha's beene used to a darke roome, and darke Clothes, and his eyes dazzle at a Satin Suite. The Hermitage of his Study, ha's made him somewhat uncouth in the world, and men make him worse by staring on him. Thus is he silly and ridiculous,

& it continues with him for some quarter of a yeere, out of the Vniversitie. But practise him a little in men, and brush him o're with good company, and hee shall out-ballance those glisterers as farre as a solid substance do's a feather, or Gold Gold-lace.

34. A HIGH SPIRITED MAN

IS one that lookes like a proud man, but is not: you may forgive him his lookes for his worth sake, for they are only too proud to be base. One whom no rate can buy off from the least piece of his freedome, and make him disgest an unworthy thought an houre. Hee cannot crouch to a great man to possesse him, nor fall low to the earth, to rebound never so high againe. Hee stands taller on his owne bottome, then others on the advantage ground of fortune, as having solidly that honour, of which Title is but the pompe. Hee does homage to no man for his great styles sake, but is strictly just in the exaction of respect againe, and will not bate you a Complement. He is more sensible of a neglect then an undoing, and scornes no man so much as his surly threatner. A man quickly fired, and quickly layd downe with satisfaction, but remits any injury sooner then words. Onely to himselfe he is irreconcileable, whom hee never forgives a disgrace, but is still stabbing himselfe with the thought of it, and no disease that he dyes of sooner. He is one had rather perish, then be beholding for his life, and strives more to bee quitte with his friend then his enemy. Fortune may kill him, but not deject him, nor make him fall into an humbler key then before, but he is now loftier then ever in his owne defence, you shal heare him talke still after thousands; and he becomes it better, then those that have it. One that is above the World and its drudgery, and cannot pull downe his thoughts to the pelting businesses of life. He would sooner accept the Gallowes then a meane trade, or any thing that might disparage the height of man in him, and yet thinkes no death comparably base to hanging neither. One that will doe nothing upon commaund, though hee would doe it otherwise: and if ever he doe evill, it is when he is dar'd to it. He is one that if fortune equall his worth puts a luster in all preferment, but if otherwise hee bee too much crost, turnes desperately melancholy, and scornes mankind.

35. A PLAINE COUNTRY FELLOW

IS one that manures his ground wel, but lets himselfe lie fallow and untill'd. Hee ha's reason enough to doe his businesse, & not enough to be idle or melancholy. Hee seemes to have the punishment of Nabuchad-nezzar: for his conversation is among beasts, and his tallons none of the shortest, onely he eates not grasse, because he loves not sallets. His hand guides the Plough, and the Plough his thoughts, and his ditch and Land-marke is the very mound of his meditations. He expostulates with his Oxen very understandingly, and speakes Gee and Ree better then English. His mind is not much distracted with objects : but if a good fat Cowe come in his way, he stands dumbe and astonisht, and though his haste bee never so great, will fixe here hafe an houres contemplation. His habitation is some poore Thatcht roofe distinguisht from his Barne, by the loope-holes that let out smoak, which the raine had long since washt thorow, but for the double seeling of Bacon on the inside which has hung there from his Grandsires time, and is yet to make rashers for posterity. His Dinner is his other worke, for he sweats at it as much as at his labour ; he is a terrible fastner on a piece of Beefe, and you may hope to stave the Guard off sooner. His religion is a part of his Copy-hold, which hee takes from his Land-lord, and referres it wholly to his discretion. Yet if hee give him leave, he is a good Christian to his power (that is) comes to Church in his best clothes, and sits there with his Neighbours, where he is capable onely of two Prayers, for raine, & faire weather. Hee apprehends Gods blessings onely in a Good Yeere, or a fat pasture, and never prayses him but on good ground. Sunday he esteemes a day to make merry in, and thinkes a Bag-pipe as essentiall to it, as Evening-Prayer, where hee walkes very solemnly after service with his hands coupled behinde him, & censures the dauncing of his parish. His complement with his Neighbour, is a good thumpe on the backe; and his salutation, commonly some blunt Curse. Hee thinkes nothing to be vices but Pride & all ill husbandry, from which he will gravely disswade the youth and ha's some thrifty Hobnayle Proverbes to Clout his discourse. He is a niggard all the Weeke except onely Market-day, where if his Corne sell well, hee thinkes he may be drunke with a good Conscience. His feete never stinke so unbecommingly, as when hee trots after a Lawyer in Westminster-hall, and even cleaves the ground with hard scraping, in beseeching his Worship to take his money. Hee is sensible of no calamity but the burning of a Stacke of Corne, or the overflowing of a Medow, and thinkes Noahs Flood the greatest Plague that ever was, not because it Drowned the World, but spoyl'd the grasse. For Death hee is never troubled, and if he get in but his Harvest before, let it come when it will, he cares not.

36.   A MEERE GULL CITIZEN

IS one much about the same modell, and pitch of braine that the Clowne is, only of somewhat a more polite,& fynicall Ignorance, and as sillily scornes him, as he is sillily admir'd by him. The quality of the City hath affoorded him some better dresse of cloathes and language, which he uses to the best advantage, and is so much the more ridicu-lous. His chiefe education is the visits of his Shop, where if Courtiers, and fine Ladies resort, hee is infected with so much more eloquence, and if he catch one word extra-ordinary, weares it for ever. You shal heare him mince a complement sometimes that

was never made for him : and no man payes
dearer for good words, for he is oft payed
with them.   He is suted rather fine, then
in the fashion, and ha's still something to
distinguish him from a Gentleman, though
his doublet cost more : especially on Sundayes, Bridegroome-like, where he carries
the state of a very solemne man, and keepes
his Pew as his Shop : and it is a great part
of his devotion, to feast the Minister.   But
his chiefest guest is a Customer, which is the
greatest relation he acknowledges; especially,
if you be an honest Gentleman, that is, trust
him to coozen you enough.   His friendships
are a kinde of Gossiping friendships, and
those commonly within the circle of his
Trade, wherein he is carefull principally
to avoyd two things, that is poore men, and
suretyships.   He is a man will spend his
six-pence with a great deale of imputation,
and no man makes more of a pinte of Wine
then he.   He is one beares a pretty kind of
foolish love to Schollers, and to Cambridge
especially for Sturbridge Faires sake : and
of these all are trewants to him that are not
preachers, and of these the lowdest the best :
and he is much ravisht with the noyse of a
rolling tongue. He loves to heare discourses
out of his Element, and the lesse hee under-

stands, the better pleas'd, which he expresses
in a smile, and some fond Protestation. One
that do's nothing without his chuck, that is,
his Wife, with whom he is billing still in
conspiracy, and the wantoner she is, the
more power shee ha's over him: and shee
never stoopes so low after him, but is the
onely woman goes better of a Widdow then
a Maide. In the education of his child no
man fearefuller, and the danger he feares,
is a harsh schoolemaster, to whom he is
alleaging still the weakenes of the boy, and
payes a fine extraordinary for his mercy.
The first whipping rids him to the Vniversity, and from thence rids him againe
for feare of starving, and the best he makes
of him is some Gull in plush. He is one
loves to heare the famous acts of Citizens,
whereof the guilding of the Crosse hee
counts the glory of this age: and the foure
Prentises of London above all the Nine
Worthies. He intitles himselfe to all the
merits of his Company, whether Schooles,
Hospitall or exhibitions, in which hee is
joynt benefactor, though foure hundred
yeeres agoe and upbraides them farre more
then those that gave them; yet with all this
folly he ha's wit enough to get wealth, & in
that a sufficienter man, then he that is wiser.

37. A LASCIVIOUS MAN

IS the servant, he sayes, of many Mistresses, but all are but his lust : to which onely hee is faithfull, and none besides, and spends his best blood, and spirits in the service. His soule is the Bawde to his body, and those that assist him in this nature, the neerest to it. No man abuses more the name of love, or those whom hee applies this name to : for his love is like his stomacke to feed on what he loves, and the end of it to surfet and loath : till a fresh appetite rekindle him : and it kindles on any sooner, then who deserve best of him. There is a great deale of malignity in this vice, for it loves stil to spoile the best things and a virgin sometimes rather then beauty, because the undoing here is greater, and consequently his glory. No man laughs more at his sinne then hee, or is so extremely tickled with the remembrance of it : and he is more violence to a modest eare, then to her he deflowrd. A bawdy jest enters deepe into him, and whatsoever you speak, he will draw to bawdry, and his witte is never so good as here. His unchastest part is his tongue, for that commits alwayes, what hee must act seldomer:

and that commits with all, which he acts with few : for he is his own worst reporter, and men beleeve as bad of him, and yet doe not beleeve him. Nothing harder to his perswasion, then a chaste man, no Eunuch, and makes a scoffing miracle at it, if you tell him of a maide. And from this mistrust it is that such men feare marriage, or at least marry such as are of bodies to be trusted, to whom onely they sell that lust which they buy of others, and make their wife a revenew to their Mistris. They are men not easily reformed, because they are so little ill-perswaded of their illnesse, & have such pleas from Man and Nature. Besides it is a jeering, and flouting vice, and apt to put jests on the reproover. The pox onely converts them, and that onely when it kills them.

38.   A PLAYER

HE knows the right use of the World, wherein he comes to play a part & so away. His life is not idle, for it is an Action, and no man need be more wary in his doings, for the eyes of all men are upon him. His profession ha's in it a kind of contradiction, for none is more dislik'd, and yet none

more applauded, & hee ha's this misfortune
of some Scholler, too much witte makes him
a foole.   He is like our painting Gentlewomen, seldome in his owne face, seldomer
in his cloathes, and hee pleases, the better
hee counterfeits, except onely when hee is
disguised with straw for gold lace.   Hee
do's not only personate on the Stage, but
sometime in the street: for he is mask'd still
in the habite of a Gentleman.   His parts
finde him oathes and good words, which he
keepes for his use and Discourse, and makes
shew with them of a fashionable companion.
He is tragicall on the Stage, but rampant
in the Tyring-house, and sweares oathes
there which he never cond.   The waiting-
women Spectators are over-eares in love with
him, and Ladies send for him to act in their
Chambers.   Your Innes of Court men were
undone but for him, hee is their chiefe guest
and imployment, and the sole businesse that
makes them Afternoones men; The Poet only
is his Tyrant, and hee is bound to make
his friends friend drunk at his charges.
Shrove-tuesday hee feares as much as the
Bawds, and Lent is more damage to him
then the Butcher.   He was never so much
discredited as in one Act, and that was of
Parliament, which gives Hostlers Priviledge

before him, for which hee abhors it more then a corrupt Iudge. But to give him his due, one wel-furnisht Actor ha's enough in him for five common Gentlemen, and if he have a good body for sixe, and for resolution, hee shall challenge any Cato, for it ha's beene his practice to dye bravely.

39. A DETRACTOR

IS one of a more cunning & active envie, wherewith he gnaws not foolishly himselfe, but throwes it abroad, and would have it blister others. He is commonly some weake-parted fellow, and worse minded, yet is strangely ambitious to match others, not by mounting their worth, but bringing them downe with his Tongue to his owne poore-nesse. Hee is indeed like the red Dragon that pursued the woman, for when he cannot overreach another, hee opens his mouth, and throwes a flood after to drowne him. You cannot anger him worse, then to do well, & hee hates you more bitterly for this, then if you had cheated him of his patrimony with your owne discredit: He is alwayes slighting the generall opinion, and wondring why such and such men should bee applauded. Commend a good Divine, he cryes Postilling;

a Philologer, Pedantry; a Poet, Ryming; a Schooleman, dull wrangling; a sharpe conceit, Boy-ishnesse; an honest man, Plausibility. Hee comes to publike things not to learne but to catch; and if there bee but one solœcisme, that's all hee carryes away. Hee lookes on all things with a prepared sowrenesse, and is still furnish't with a Pish before hand, or some musty proverbe that disrelishes al things whatsoever. If the feare of the company make him second a commendation, it is like a Law-writ, alwayes with a clause of exception, or to smooth the way to some greater scandall. He will grant you something, and bate more; and this bating shal in conclusion take away all hee grante. His speech concludes still with an Oh but, and I could wish one thing amended; and this one thing shal be enough to deface all his former commendations. Hee will bee very inward with a man to fish some bad out of him, and make his slanders hereafter more authenticke, when it is said a friend repeated it. Hee will invegle you to naughtinesse, to get your good name into his clutches, and make you drunk to shew you reeling. He passes the more plausibly, because all men have a smatch of his humour, and it is thought freenes which

68

is malice. If he can say nothing of a man, hee will seeme to speak riddles, as if he could tel strange stories if he would : and when he ha's rackt his invention to the uttermost, hee ends : But I wish him well, and therefore must hold my peace. He is always listning and enquiring after men, and suffers not a cloake to passe by him unexamin'd. In briefe, hee is one that ha's lost all good himselfe, and is loth to finde it in another.

40. A RASH MAN

IS a man too quicke for himselfe: one whose actions put a leg still before his judgement, and out-run it. Every hot fancy or passion is the signall that sets him forward : and his reason comes still in the reare. One that ha's braine enough, but not patience to disgest a businesse, and stay the leasure of a second thought. All deliberation is to him a kinde of sloth, and freezing of action, and it shall burn him rather then take cold. He is alwaies resolv'd at first thinking, and the ground he goes upon is hap what may. Thus hee enters not, but throwes himselfe violently upon all things, and for the most part is as violently upon all off againe : and as an obstinate I will was the preface to his undertaking : so his conclusion is commonly I would I had not, for such men seldome do any thing that they are not forc'd to take in pieces againe, and are so much furder off from doing it, as they have done already. His friends are with him as his Physicians : sought to onely in his sicknesse, and extremity, and to helpe him out of that mire he ha's plungd himselfe into, for in the suddennesse of his passions hee would heare nothing, and now his ill successe ha's allayd him, hee heares too late. He is a man still swayed with the first reports, and no man more in the power of a pickthank then he. He is one will fight first, and then expostulate ; condemne first, and then examine. He loses his friend in a fitt of quarrelling, & in a fitt of kindnesse undoes himselfe : And then curses the occasion drew this mischiefe upon him, and cryes God mercy for it, and curses againe. His Repentance is meerly a rage against himselfe, and hee does something in it selfe to be repented againe. Hee is a man whom fortune must goe against much to make him happy, for had he beene suffer'd his owne way, hee had beene undone.

41. A YOUNG GENTLEMAN OF THE VNIVERSITY.

IS one that comes there to weare a gown, and to say hereafter, he ha's beene at the Vniversity. His Father sent him thither, because he heard there were the best Fencing and Dancing Schooles, from these he ha's his Education, from his Tutor the over-sight. The first Element of his knowledge is to be shewne the Colledges, and initiated in a Taverne by the way, which hereafter hee will learne of himselfe. The two markes of his seniority, is the bare Velvet of his gowne, and his proficiency at Tennis, where when hee can once play a Set, he is a Fresh-man no more. His Study ha's commonly handsome Shelves, his Bookes neate silke strings, which he shewes to his Fathers man, and is loth to untye or take downe, for feare of misplacing. Vpon foule dayes for recreation hee retyres thither, and looks over the pretty booke his Tutor Reades to him, which is commonly some short History, or a piece of Euphormio ; for which his Tutor gives him Money to spend next day. His maine loytering is at the Library, where he studies Armes and Bookes of Honour, and turnes a Gentleman-Critick in Pedigrees. Of all things hee endures not to bee mistaken for a Scholler, and hates a black suit though it bee of Satin. His companion is ordinarily some stale fellow, that ha's beene notorious for an Ingle to gold hatbands, whom he admires at first, afterward scornes. If hee have spirit or wit, hee may light of better company, and learne some flashes of wit, which may doe him Knights service in the Country hereafter. But he is now gone to the Inns of Court, where hee studies to forget, what hee learn'd before, his acquaintance and the fashion.

42.   A WEAKE MAN

IS a child at mans estate, one whom nature hudled up in haste, and left his best part unfurnish't. The rest of him is growne to bee a man, onely his braine staies behinde. He is one that ha's not improov'd his first rudiments, nor attain'd any proficiency by his stay in the world, but wee may speake of him yet, as when hee was in the budde, a good harmelesse nature, a well meaning mind, and no more. It is his misery that he now most wants a Tutor, and is too old to have one. He is two steps above a foole,

and a great many mo below a wise-man : yet
the foole is oft given him, & by those whom
hee esteemes most. Some tokens of him
are : He loves men better upon relation then
experience : for he is exceedingly enamour'd
of Strangers, and none quicklier a-weary
of his friends. Hee charges you at first
meeting with all his secrets, and on better
acquaintance growes more reserv'd. Indeed
he is one that mistakes much his abusers
for friends, and his friends for enemies,
and he apprehends your hate in nothing
so much, as in good counsell. One that is
flexible with any thing but reason, and
then onely perverse ; and you may better
intice then perswade him. A servant to
every tale and flatterer, and whom the last
man still works over. A great affecter of
wits & such pretinesses, and his company
is costly to him, for he seldome ha's it but
invited. His friendship commonly is begun
in a supper, & lost in lending money. The
Taverne is a dangerous place to him, for to
drinke and to be drunke, is with him all
one, and his braine is sooner quench't then
his thirst. He is drawne into naughtines
with company, but suffers alone, and the
Bastard commonly laid to his charge. One
that will bee patiently abus'd, and take

exceptions a Moneth after when he understands it, and then be abused again into a
reconcilement; and you cannot endeare him
more then by coozening him, and it is a
temptation to those that would not. One
discoverable in all sillinesses to all men
but himselfe, and you may take any mans
knowledge of him better then his owne.
Hee will promise the same thing to twenty,
and rather then deny one, breake with all.
One that ha's no power o're himselfe, o're
his businesse, o're his friends : but a prey
& pity to all : & if his fortunes once sinke,
men quickely cry, Alas, and forget him.

43.   A TOBACCO-SELLER

IS the onely man that findes good in it
which others brag of, but do not; for it is
meate, drinke, and clothes to him. No man
opens his ware with greater seriousnesse,
or challenges your judgement more in the
approbation. His shop is the Randevous of
spitting, where men dialogue with their noses,
& their communication is smoake. It is the
place onely where Spaine is commended, &
prefer'd before England it selfe. He should
be well experienc'd in the world : for he ha's
daily tryall of mens nostrils, and none is

better acquainted with humors. Hee is the piecing commonly of some other trade which is bawde to his Tobacco, and that to his wife, which is the flame that followes this smoke.

44. AN AFFECTED MAN

IS an extraordinary man, in ordinary things. One that would goe a straine beyond himselfe, and is taken in it. A man that overdoes all things with great solemnity of circumstance : and whereas with more negligence he might passe better, makes himselfe, with a great deale of endevour, ridiculous. The fancy of some odde quaintnesses have put him cleane beside his Nature, he cannot bee that hee would, and hath lost what he was. He is one must be point-blank in every trifle, as if his credit, & opinion hung upon it : the very space of his armes in an imbrace studied before, and premeditated : and the figure of his countenance, of a fortnights contriving. Hee will not curse you without booke, and extempore, but in some choice way, and perhaps as some Great man curses. Every action of his, cryes Doe yee marke mee ? and men doe marke him, how absurd he is. For affectation is the most betraying humour : and nothing that puzzles a man lesse to find out then this. All the actions of his life are like so many things bodg'd in without any naturall cadence, or connexion at all. You shall tracke him all thorow like a Schooleboyes Theame, one piece from one author, and this from another, and joyne all in this generall, that they are none of his owne : You shal observe his mouth not made for that tone, nor his face for that simper : And it is his lucke that his finest things most mis-become him. If he affect the Gentleman as the humour most commonly lyes that way : not the least puntilio of fine man, but hee is strict in to a haire, even to their very negligences which he cons as rules : He will not carry a knife with him to wound reputation, and pay double a reckoning, rather then ignobly question it. And he is full of this Ignobly and Nobly and Gentilely, & this meere feare to trespasse against the Gentill way, putts him out most of al. It is a humor runs thorow many things besides, but is an il-favour'd ostentation in all, and thrives not. And the best use of such men is, they are good parts in a play.

45. A POT-POET

IS the dreggs of wit ; yet mingled with good drink may have some relish. His Inspirations are more reall then others ; for they doe but faine a god, but he ha's his by him. His verse runs like the Tap, and his invention as the Barrel, ebs and flowes at the mercy of the spiggot. In thin drinke hee aspires not above a Ballad, but a cup of Sacke inflames him, & sets his Muse & Nose a fire together. The Presse is his Mint, and stampes him now & then a sixe pence or two in reward of the baser coyne his Pamphlet. His workes would scarce sell for three halfe pence, though they are given oft for three Shillings, but for the pretty Title that allures the Country Gentleman: for which the Printer maintaines him in Ale a fortnight. His verses are like his clothes miserable Cento's and patches, yet their pace is not altogether so hobbling as an Almanacks. The death of a great man, or the burning of a house furnish him with an Argument, & the nine Muses are out strait in mourning gowne, and Melpomene cryes Fire, Fire. His other Poems are but Briefs in Rime, and like the poore Greekes collections to redeeme from captivity. He is a man now much imploy'd in commendations of our Navie, and a bitter inveigher against the Spaniard. His frequent'st Workes goe out in single sheets, and are chanted from market to market, to a vile tune, and a worse throat: whil'st the poore Country wench melts like her butter to heare them. And these are the Stories of some men of Tiburne: or a strange Monster out of Germany: or sitting in a Bawdy-house, hee writes Gods Iudgements. He drops away at last in some obscure painted Cloth, to which himselfe made the Verses, and his life like a Canne too full spills, upon the bench. He leaves twenty shillings on the score, which my Hostesse loses.

46. A PLAUSIBLE MAN

IS one that would faine run an even path in the world, and jutt against no man. His endevour is not to offend, and his ayme the generall opinion. His conversation is a kinde of continued Complement, and his life a practice of manners. The relation hee beares to others, a kinde of fashionable respect, not friendship, but friendlines, which is equall to all and generall, and his kindnesses seldome exceed courtesies. Hee loves not deeper mutualities, because he would not take sides, nor hazard himselfe on displeasures, which he principally avoids. At your first acquaintance with him he is exceeding kinde and friendly, and at your twentieth meeting after, but friendly still. He ha's an excellent command over his patience & tongue, especially the last, which hee accommodates alwaies to the times and persons, and speakes seldome what is sincere, but what is civill. He is one that uses al companies, drinkes all healths, and is reasonable cool in all Religions. He considers who are friends to the company, and speakes well where hee is sure to heare of it againe. He can listen to a foolish discourse with an applausive attention, and conceale his Laughter at Non-sense. Silly men much honour and esteeme him, because by his faire reasoning with them as with men of understanding, he puts them into an erronious opinion of themselves, and makes them forwarder heereafter to their owne discovery. Hee is one rather well thought on then belov'd, and that love hee ha's, is more of whole companies together then any one in particular. Men gratifie him notwith-standing with a good report, and what-ever vices he ha's besides, yet having no enemies, he is sure to be an honest fellow.

47. A BOWLE-ALLEY

IS the place where there are three things thrown away besides Bowls, to wit, time, money and curses, and the last ten for one. The best sport in it, is the Gamesters, and he enjoyes it, that lookes on and bets not. It is the Schoole of wrangling, and worse then the Schooles, for men will cavill here for an haires breadth, and make a stirre where a straw would end the controversie. No Anticke screwes mens bodies into such strange flexures, and you would think them here senseles, to speak sense to their Bowle, and put their trust in intreaties for a good cast. The Betters are the factious noyse of the Alley, or the Gamesters Beadsmen that pray for them. They are somewhat like those that are cheated by great men, for they lose their money & must say nothing. It is the best discovery of humours, especially in the losers, where you have fine variety of impatience, whil'st some fret, som raile, some sweare, and others more ridiculously comfort themselves with Philosophy. To give you the Morall of it; It is the Embleme of the world, or the worlds ambition : where most are short, or over, or wide or wrong-

Byas't, and some few justle into the Mistris
Fortune. And it is here as in the Court,
where the neerest are most spighted, and
all blowes aym'd at the Toucher.

48. THE WORLDS WISE MAN

IS an able and sufficient wicked man, it
is a proofe of his sufficiency that hee is
not called wicked, but wise. A man wholy
determin'd in himselfe and his owne ends,
and his instrument : herein any thing that
wil doe it. His friends are a part of his
engines, and as they serve to his workes,
us'd or laid by. Indeed hee knowes not
this thing of friend, but if hee give you the
name, it is a signe he ha's a plot on you.
Never more active in his businesses, then
when they are mixt with some harme to
others : and 'tis his best play in this Game
to strike off and lie in the place. Successeful
commonly in these undertakings, because
he passes smoothly those rubs which others
stumble at, as Conscience and the like : and
gratulates himselfe much in this advantage :
Oathes and falshood he counts the neerest
way, and loves not by any meanes to goe
about. Hee ha's many fine quips at this
folly of plaine dealing, but his tush is

greatest at Religion, yet hee uses this too, and Vertue, and good Words, but is lesse dangerously a Devil then a Saint. He ascribes all honesty to an unpractis'dnesse in the World: and Conscience a thing meerely for Children. Hee scornes all that are so silly to trust him, & onely not scornes his enemy; especially if as bad as himselfe: He feares him as a man well arm'd, & provided, but sets boldly on good natures, as the most vanquishable. One that seriously admires those worst Princes, as Sforza, Borgia, and Richard the third: and cals matters of deep villany things of difficulty. To whom murthers are but resolute Acts, & Treason a businesse of great consequence. One whom two or three Countries make up to this compleatnes, and he ha's traveled for the purpose. His deepest indearment is a communication of mischiefe, & then onely you have him fast. His conclusion is commonly one of these two, either a great Man, or hang'd.

49.   A SURGEON

IS one that ha's some businesse about his Building or little house of man whereof Nature is as it were the Tyler, and hee the

Playsterer. It is ofter out of reparations, then an old Parsonage, and then he is set on worke to patch it againe. Hee deales most with broken Commodities, as a broken Head or a mangled face; and his gaines are very ill got; for he lives by the hurts of the Common-wealth. He differs from a Physician as a sore do's from a disease, or the sicke from those that are not whole, the one distempers you within, the other blisters you without. He complaines of the decay of Valour in these dayes, and sighes for that slashing Age of Sword and Buckler; and thinkes the Law against Duels, was made meerly to wound his Vocation. Hee had beene long since undone, if the charity of the Stewes had not relieved him, from whom he ha's his Tribute as duely as the Pope, or a wind-fall sometimes from a Taverne, if a quart Pot hit right. The rarenesse of his custome makes him pitilesse when it comes: and he holds a patient longer then our Courts a Cause. Hee tells you what danger you had beene in, if hee had staid but a minute longer; and though it bee but a prickt finger, he makes of it much matter. He is a reasonable cleanely man, considering the Scabs hee ha's to deale with, and your finest Ladyes now and then are beholding to him for their best dressings. Hee curses old Gentlewomen, and their charity that makes his Trade their Almes, but his envie is never stir'd so much, as when Gentlemen goe over to fight upon Calice Sands : whom hee wishes drown'd e're they come there, rather then the French shall get his Custome.

50.   A PROPHANE MAN

IS one that denies God as farre as the Law gives him leave, that is, onely does not say so in downe-right Termes, for so farre hee may goe. A man that does the greatest sinnes calmely, and as the ordinary actions of life, and as calmely discourses of it againe. He will tell you his businesse is to breake such a Commandement, and the breaking of the Commandement shall tempt him to it. His words are but so many vomitings cast up to the lothsomenesse of the hearers, onely those of his company loath it not. Hee will take upon him with oathes to pelt some tenderer man out of his company, and makes good sport at his conquest o're the Puritan foole. The Scripture supplies him for jests, and hee reades it of purpose to bee thus merry. He will proove you his sin out of the Bible, and then aske if you

will not take that Authority : He never sees
the Church but of purpose to sleepe in
it : or when some silly man preaches with
whom he means to make sport, and is most
jocund in the Church. One that nick-names
Clergymen with all the termes of reproch,
as Rat, Black-coate, & the like which he will
be sure to keepe up, & never calls them by
other. That sings Psalms when he is drunke,
and cryes God mercy in mockery ; for hee
must doe it. Hee is one seemes to dare God
in all his actions, but indeed would out-dare
the opinion of him, which would else turne
him desperate : for Atheisme is the refuge
of such sinners, whose repentance would
bee onely to hang them selves.

51.   A CONTEMPLATIVE MAN

IS a Scholer in this great Vniversity the
World ; and the fame, his Booke and Study.
Hee cloysters not his Meditations in the
narrow darkenesse of a Roome, but sends
them abroad with his eyes, and his Braine
travells with his Feet. He lookes upon
Man from a high Tower, and sees him
trulyer at this distance in his Infirmities &
poorenesse. He scornes to mixe himselfe
in mens actions, as he would to act upon

a Stage, but sits aloft on the Scaffold a censuring Spectator. Hee will not lose his time by being busie, nor make so poore a use of the world, as to hug and embrace it. Nature admits him as a partaker of her Sports, and askes his approbation as it were of her owne Workes, and uariety. Hee comes not in Company, because hee would not be solitary, but findes Discourse enough with himselfe, and his owne thoughts are his excellent play-fellowes. Hee lookes not upon a thing as a yawning stranger at novelties; but his search is more mysterious and inward, and hee spels Heaven out of earth. He knits his observations together, and makes a Ladder of them all to climbe to God. He is free from uice, because he ha's no ocasion to imploy it, and is above those ends that makes men wicked. He ha's learnt all can heere bee taught him, and comes now to Heaven to see more.

52.   A SHE PRECISE HYPOCRITE.

IS one in whome good Women suffer, and have their truth mis-interpreted by her folly. She is one, she knowes not what her selfe if you aske her, but she is indeed one that ha's taken a toy at the fashion of religion,

and is enamour'd of the New-fangle. Shee
is a Nonconformist in a close Stomacher
and Ruffe of Geneva Print, and her puritie
consists much in her Linnen. She ha's
heard of the Rag of Rome, and thinkes it
a uery sluttish Religion, and rayles at the
Whore of Babilon for a uery naughty Woman.
Shee ha's left her Virginity as a Relique of
Popery, and marries in her Tribe without
a Ring. Her devotion at the Church is
much in the turning up of her eye ; and
turning downe the leafe in her Booke, when
shee heares nam'd Chapter and Verse. When
shee comes home, shee commends the Sermon
for the Scripture, and two houres. She
loves preaching better then praying, and of
Prachers, Lecturers, and thinkes the Weeke
dayes Exercise farre more edyfying then
the Sundayes. Her oftest Gossippings are
Sabbath-dayes iourneyes, where (though an
enemy to superstition) shee will goe in
Pilgrimage five mile to a silenc'd Minister,
when there is a better Sermon in her owne
Parish. Shee doubts of the Virgin Marie's
Salvation, and dares not Saint her, but
knowes her owne place in heaven as per-
fectly, as the Pew shee ha's a key to. She
is so taken up with Faith, shee ha's no
roome for Charity, and undestands no good

Workes, but what are wrought on the Sampler. Shee accounts nothing Vices but Superstition, and an Oath, and thinkes Adultery a lesse sinne, then to sweare by my Truely. Shee rayles at other Women by the names of Iezabel and Dalilah : & calls her owne daughters Rebecca and Abigal, and not Anne but Hannah. Shee suffers them not to learne on the Virginals, because of their affinitie with the Organs, but is reconcil'd to the Bells for the Chymes sake, since they were reform'd to the tune of a Psalm. She overflowes so with the Bible, that shee spils it upon every occasion, & will not Cudgell her Maides without Scripture. It is a question whether she is more troubled with the Divel, or the Divell with her : she is always challenging and daring him, and her weapon is the Practice of Piety. Nothing angers her so much, as that Women cannot preach, and in this point onely thinkes the Brownist erroneous: but what shee cannot at the Church, shee does at the Table, where she prattles more then any against sense, and Antichrist, till a Capons wing silence her. She expounds the Priests of Baal, reading Ministers, and thinkes the Salvation of that Parish as desperate as the Turkes. She is a maine derider to her capacitie of those that are not her Preachers, and censures all Sermons but bad ones. If her Husband be a Tradesman, she helpes him to customers, howsoever to good cheere, and they are a most faithfull couple at these meetings : for they never faile. Her Conscience is like others. Lust never satsfied, and you might better answer Scotus then her Scruples. Shee is one that thinkes shee performes all her duty to God in hearing, and shewes the fruites of it in talking. Shee is more fiery against the May-pole then her Husband, & thinkes hee might doe a Phineas his act to break the pate of the Fiddler. She is an everlasting Argument ; but I am weary of her.

53. A SCEPTICKE IN RELIGION.

IS one that hangs in the ballance with all sorts of opinions, whereof not one but stirres him, and none swayes him. A man guiltier of credulity then hee is taken to bee ; for it is out of his beleefe of every thing, that hee fully beleeves nothing. Each Religion scarres him from it's contrary : none perswades him to it selfe. Hee would be wholly a Christian, but that he is something of an Atheist, and wholly an Atheist, but that hee is partly a

Christian ; and a perfect Heretick, but that there are so many to distract him.   He findes reason in all opinions, truth in none : indeed the least reason perplexes him, and the best will not satisfie him.   Hee is at most a confus'd and wilde Christian, not specializ'd by any forme but capable of all.   He uses the Lands Religion, because it is next him, yet he sees not why he may not take the other, but he chuses this, not as better, but because there is not a pin to choose. He finds doubts and scruples better then resolves them, and is alwayes too hard for himselfe.   His learning is too much for his braine ; and his iudgment too little for his lerning, & his over-opinion of both spoiles all.   Pity it was his mischance of being a scholler ; for it do's only distract and irregulate him and the world by him. He hammers much in generall upon our opinions uncertainty, and the possibility of erring makes him not uenture on what is true.   Hee is troubled at this naturalnesse of Religion to Countries, that Protestantisme should bee borne so in England, and Popery abroad, and that fortune and the Starres should so much share in it.   He likes not this connexion of the Common-weale, and Divinity, and feares it may be an Archpractice of State. In our differences with Rome he is strangely unfix't, and a new man every new day, as his last discourse, Books, Meditations transport him. Hee could like the gray haires of Popery, did not some dotages there stagger him, he would come to us sooner, but our new name affrights him. He is taken with their Miracles, but doubts an imposture; he conceives of our Doctrine better; but it seemes too empty and naked. Hee cannot drive into his fancy the circumscription of Truth to our corner, and is as hardly perswaded to thinke their old Legends true. He approves wel of our Faith, and more of their workes, and is sometimes much affected at the zeale of Amsterdam. His conscience interposes it selfe betwixt Duellers, and whilst it would part both, is by both wounded. He wil somtimes propend much to us upon the reading a good Writer, and at Bellarmine recoiles as farre backe againe, and the Fathers iustle him from one side to another. Now Sosinus and Vorstius afresh torture him, and he agrees with none worse then himselfe. Hee puts his foot into Heresies tenderly as a Cat in the water, and pulls it out againe, and still something unanswer'd delayes, yet him he beares away some parcel of each,

and you may sooner pick all Religions out
of him then one. He cannot thinke so many
wise men should be in error, nor so many
honest men out of the way and his wonder
is doubled, when he sees these oppose one
another. Hee hates autority as the Tyrant of
reason, & you cannot anger him worse then
with a Fathers dixit, & yet that many are not
perswaded with reason, shall authorize this
doubt. In sum, his whole life is a question,
and his salvation a greater, which death only
concludes, and then hee is resolu'd.

54. AN ATTURNEY.

HIS Ancient beginning was a blue coat,
since a livery, and his haching under a
Lawyer ; whence though but pen-feather'd,
hee hath now nested for himself, and with
his hoorded pence purchast an Office. Two
Deskes, and a quire of paper set him up,
where he now sits in state for all commers.
Wee can call him no great Author, yet hee
writes uery much and with the infamy of
the Court is maintain'd in his Libels. Hee
ha's some smatch of a Scholler, and yet uses
Latine uery hardly, and lest it should accuse
him, cuts it off in the midst and will not let
it speake out. He is contrary to great men,

maintained by his followers, that is, his poore country Clients, that worship him more then their Landlord, and be they never such churles, he lookes for their courtesie. He first racks them soundly himselfe, & then delivers them to the Lawier for execution. His looks are uery solicitous, importing much haste and dispatch, he is never without his hands full of businesse, that is, of paper. His skin becomes at last as dry as his parchment, and his face as intricate as the most winding cause. He talkes Statutes as fiercely, as if he had mooted seven yeers in the Inns of Court; when all his skil is stucke in his girdle, or in his office window. Strife and wrangling have made him rich, and he is thankefull to his benefactor, and nourishes it. If he live in a Country uillage, he makes all his neighbours good Subiects; for there shall be nothing done but what there is law for. His businesse gives him not leave to thinke of his conscience & when the time, or terme of his life is going out, for Doomes-day he is secure, for hee hopes hee ha's a tricke to reverse iudgment.

55. A COWARD.

IS the man that is commonly most fierce
agaist the Coward, and labouring to take
off this suspition from himselfe: for the
opinion of ualour is a good protection to
those that dare not use it. No man is
ualianter then he in civill company, and
where he thinkes no danger may come on
it, and is the readiest man to fall upon a
drawer, & those that must not strike againe.
Wonderfull exceptious and cholerick where
he sees men are loth to give him occasion,
and you cannot pacify him better then by
quarrelling with him. The hotter you grow,
the more temperate man is hee, he protests
hee alwaies honour'd you, and the more you
raile upon him, the more he honours you,
and you threaten him at last into a uery
honest quiet man. The sight of a sword
wounds him more sensibly then the stroke,
for before that come hee is dead already.
Every man is his master that dare beate
him, and every man dares that knowes him.
And he that dare doe this, is the only man
can doe much with him: for his friend hee
cares not for, as a man that carries no such
terror as his enemy, which for this cause

only is more potent with him of the two. And men fall out with him of purpose to get courtesies from him, and be brib'd againe to a reconcilement. A man in whome no secret can bee bound up, for the apprehension of each danger loosens him, and makes him bewray both the roome and it. Hee is a Christian meerely for feare hell of fire, and if any Religion could fright him more, would bee of that.

56.   A PARTIALL MAN.

IS the opposite extreme to a Defamer, for the one speakes ill falsely, and the other well, and both slander the truth. Hee is one that is still weighing men in the scale of Comparisons, and puts his affection in the one ballance and that swayes. His friend alwayes shall doe best, and you shal rarely heare good of his enemy. Hee considers first the man, and then the thing, and restraines all merit to what they deserve of him. Commendations hee esteemes not the debt of Worth, but the requitall of kindnesse : and if you aske his reason, shewes his interest, and tells you how much hee is beholding to that Man. Hee is one that ties his iudgment to the Wheele of Fortune, & they determine giddily both alike. He preferres England before other countries, because he was borne there, and Oxford before other Vniversities, because hee was brought up there, and the best Scholler there, is one of his owne Colledge and the best Scholler there is one of his friends. Hee is a great favourer of great persons, and his argument is still that which should be Antecedent, as he is in high place, therefore uertuous, he is prefer'd, therefore worthy. Never aske his opinion, for you shall heare but his faction, & he is indifferent in nothing but Conscience. Men esteeme him for this a zealous affectionate, but they mistake him many times, for he does it but to bee esteem'd so. Of all men he is worst to write an Historie, for hee will praise a Seianus or Tiberius, and for some pettie respect of his, all posterity shall bee cozend.

57. A TRUMPETER.

IS the Elephant with the great Trunke, for hee eates nothing but what comes through this way. His Profession is not so worthy as to occasion insolence, and yet no man so much puft up. His face is as Brazen as his Trumpet, and (which is worse) as a

Fiddlers, from whom he differeth onely in this, that his impudence is dearer. The Sea of Drinke, and much wind make a storme perpetually in his Cheeks, and his looke is like his noyse, blustering and tempestuous. Hee was whilome the sound of Warre, but now of Peace; yet as terrible as ever, for whereso ere he comes, they are sure to pay for't. He is the common attendant of glittering folkes, whether in the Court or Stage, where he is alwaies the prologues prologue. He is somewhat in the nature of a Hogshed shrillest when he is empty; when his belly is full, hee is quiet enough. No man proves life more to bee a blast, or himselfe a bubble & hee is like a counterfeit Bankrupt, thrives best when he is blowne up.

58. A VULGAR-SPIRITED MAN.

IS one of the heard of World. One that followes meerely the common crye, and makes it louder by one. A man that loves none but who are publikely affected, and hee will not be wiser then the rest of the Towne. That never ownes a friend after an ill name, or some generall imputation, though he knowes it most unworthy. That opposes to reason, Thus men say, and thus most doe, & thus the world goes, & thinkes this enough to poyse the other. That worship men in place, and those onely, and thinkes all a great man speakes, Oracles. Much taken with my Lords iest, and repeates you it all to a syllable. One that iustifies nothing out of fashion, nor any opinion out of the applauded way, that thinkes certainly all Spaniards and Iesuites uery uillaines, and is still cursing the Pope and Spinola. One that thinkes the gravest Cassocke the best Scholler: and the best Clothes the finest man. That is taken onely with broad and obscœne wit, and hisses any thing to deepe for him. That cryes Chaucer for his Money above all our English Poets: because the uoice ha's gone so, and hee ha's read none. That is much ravisht with such a Noble mans courtesie, and would uenture his life for him, because he put off his Hat. One that is formost still to kisse the Kings hand, and cryes God blesse his Maiestie loudest. That rayles on all men condemn'd and out of favour, and the first that sayes away with the Traytors: yet struck with much ruth at Executions, and for pittie to see a man die, could kill the Hangman. That comes to London to see it, and the pretty things in it, and the chiefe cause of his iourney the Beares : That measures the happines of the Kingdome be the cheapnes of corne ; and conceives no harme of State, but il trading. Within this compasse too, come those that are too much wedg'd into the world, and have no lifting thoughts above those things ; that call to thrive well, to doe well, and preferment only the grace of God. That ayme all Studies at this marke, and shew you poore Schollers as an example to take heed by. That thinke the Prison and want, a Iudgement for some sinne, and never like well hereafter of a Iayle-bird. That know no other content but wealth, bravery, and the Towne-pleasures ; that thinke all else but idle speculation, and the Philosophers, mad-men. In short, men that are carried away with all outward-nesses, shewes, appearances, the streame ; the people ; for there is no man of worth but has a piece of singularity, and scornes something.

59. A PLODDING STUDENT.

IS a kind of Alchymist or Pesecuter of Nature, that would change the dull lead of his brain into finer mettle with successe many times as unprosperous, or at least not quitting the cost, to witte, of his owne Oyle and Candles. He ha's a strange forc't appetite to Learning, and to atchive it brings, nothing but patience and a body. His Study is not great but continuall, and consists much in the sitting up till after midnight in a rug gowne, and a Night-cap, to the uanquishing perhaps of some sixe lines: yet what he ha's, he ha's perfect, for he reads it so long to understand it, till he gets it without Booke. Hee may with much industry make a breach into Logicke, and arive at some ability in an Argument: but for politer Studies hee dare not skirmish with them, and for poetry accounts it impregnable. His Invention is no more then the finding out of his papers, and his few gleanings there, and his disposition of them is as iust as the bookbinders, a setting or glewing of them together. Hee is a great discomforter of young students, by telling them what travell it h'as cost him, and how often his braine turn'd at Philosophy, and makes others feare studying as a cause of Duncery. Hee is a man much given to apothegms which serve him for wit, & seldome breakes any Iest, but which belong'd to some Lacedemonian or Romane in Lycosthenes. Hee is like a dull Cariers horse, that wil goe a whole weeke together but never out of a foot-pace : & hee that sets forth on the Saturday shall overtake him.

60.   A SORDID RICH MAN.

IS a begger of a faire estate : of whose wealth wee may say as of other mens vn-thriftinesse, that it ha's brought him to this: when he had nothing, hee liv'd in another kind of fashion. He is a man whom men hate in his owne behalfe, for using himselfe thus, and yet being upon himselfe, it is but iustice ; for he deserves it. Euery accession of a fresh heape bates him so much of his allowance, and brings him a degree neerer starving. His body had beene long since desperate, but for the reparation of other mens tables, where hee hoords meate in his belly for a moneth, to maintaine him in hunger so long. His clothes were never young in our memorie : you might make long Epocha's from them, and put them into the Almanack with the deare yeare, and the great frost, and he is knowne by them longer then his face. He is one never gave almes in his life, & yet is as charitable to his Neighbour as himselfe. Hee will redeeme a penny with his reputation, and lose all his friends to boote : & his reason, is he will not be undone. He never payes any thing, but with strictnesse of law, for feare of which onely he steales not. Hee loves to pay short a shilling or two in a great sum, and is glad to gaine that, when he can no more. He never sees friend but in a iourney to save the charges of an Inne, and then onely is not sicke : and his friends never see him, but to abuse him. He is a fellow indeed of a kind of frantick thrift, and one of the strangest things that wealth can worke.

61.   PAULS WALKE.

IS the Lands Epitome, or you may cal it the lesser Ile of Great Brittaine. It is more then this, the whole worlds Map, which you may heere discerne in it's perfect'st motion iustling and turning. It is a heape of stones & men, with a vast confusion of Languages, and were the Steeple not sanctified, nothing liker Babel. The noyse in it is like that of Bees, a strange humming of buzze-mixt of walking tongues and feete : It is a kinde of still roare or loud whisper. It is the great Exchange of all discourse, and no busines whatsoever but is here stirring and a foote. It is the Synod of all pates politicke, ioynted & laid together in most serious posture, & they are not halfe so busie at the Parliament. It is the Anticke of tailes to tailes, & backes to backes, and for vizards you need goe no further then faces. It is the Market of young Lecturers, whom you may cheapen here at all rates and sizes. It is the generall Mint of al famous lies, which are here like the legends of Popery, first coyn'd and stampt in the Church. All inventions are emptyed heere, and not few pockets. The best signe of a Temple in it is, that it is the Theeves Sanctuary, which robbe more safely in the Croud, then a wildernesse, whilst every searcher is a bush to hide them. It is the other expence of the day, after Playes, Taverne, and a Bawdy-House, and men have still some Oathes left to sweare heere. It is the eares Brothell, & satisfies their lust, & ytch. The Visitants are all men without exceptions, but the principall Inhabitants

& possessors, are stale Knights, & Captaines Out of service, men of long Rapiers, and Breeches, which after all, turne Merchants heere and traffick for Newes. Some make it a preface to their Dinner, and travell for a Stomacke: but thriftier men make it their Ordinarie: and boord heere uery cheape. Of all such places, it is least haunted with Hobgoblins, for if a Ghost would walke more, hee could not.

62. A MEERE GREAT MAN.

IS so much Heraldrie without honour: himselfe lesse reall then his Title. His uertue is that hee was his Fathers son, and all the expectation of him to beget another. A man that lives meerely to preserve anothers memorie, and let us know who died so many yeares agoe. One of iust as much use as his Images: onely he differs in this that hee can speake himselfe, and save the fellow of Westminster a labour: and hee remembers nothing better then what was out of his life: His Grandfather and their acts are his discourse, and he tells them with more glory then they did them, and it is well they did enough, or els he had wanted matter. His other studies are his sports

and those uices that are fit for Great men.
Every uanity of his ha's his officer, and is
a serious imployment for his servants. Hee
talkes loud and baudily, and scurvily, as
a part of state, and they heare him with
reverence. All good qualities are below
him, and especially learning except some
parcels of the Chronicle, and the writing
of his name, which hee learnes to write, not
to be read. Hee is meerely of his servants
faction & their instrument for their friends
and enemies, and is alwaies least thankt for
his owne courtesies. They that foole him
most, doe most with him, & he little thinkes
how many laugh at him, barehead. No man
is kept in ignorance more of himselfe and
men, for he heares nought but flatterie, and
what is fit to be spoken : truth with so much
preface, that it loses it selfe. Thus hee lives
till his Tombe be made ready, and is then
a grave Statue to posterity.

63.   A COOKE.

THE Kitchin is his Hell and hee the
Divell in it, where his meate and he fry
together. His Revennues are showr'd downe
from the fat of the Land, and he enterlards
his owne grease among to help the drippings.

Cholericke he is, not by nature so much as his Art, & it is a shrewd temptation that the chopping knife is so neere. His weapons ofter offensive, are a messe of hotte broth and scalding water, and woe be to him that comes in his way. In the Kitchin he will domineere, and rule the roste, in spight of his Master, & curses in the uery Dialect of his Calling. His labour is meere blustring & furie, & his Speech like that of Sailers in a storme, a thousand businesses at once, yet in all this tumult hee do's not love combustion, but will bee the first man that shall goe and quench it. He is never good Christian till a hizzing Pott of Ale ha's flak't him, like Water cast on a firebrand, and for that time he is tame and dispossest. His cunning is not small in Architecture, for he builds strange Fabricks in Paste, Towres & Castles, which are offered to the assault of ualiant teeth & like Darius his Palace in one Banquet demolisht. He is a pittilesse murderer of Innocents, and he mangles poore soules with unheard of tortures, and it is thought the Martyrs persecutions were devised from hence, sure we are, Saint Lawrence his Gridiron came out of his Kitchin. His best facultie is at the Dresser, where hee seemes to have great skill in the Tactikes, ranging his Dishes in order Militarie: and placing with great discretion in the forefront meates more strong and hardy, and the more cold and cowardly in the reare, as quaking Tarts, and quivering Custards, and such milke-sop Dishes which scape many times the fury of the encounter. But now the second Course is gone up, and he downe into the Seller, where he drinks and sleeps till foure a clocke in the afternoone, and then returnes againe to his Regiment.

64.   A BOLD FORWARD MAN

IS a lustie fellow in a crow'd, that's beholding more to his elbow then his leggs, for he do's not goe but thrusts well. Hee is a good shufler in the world, wherein he is so soft putting forth, that at length he puts on. He can doe some things but dare doe much more, and is like a desperate soldier, who will assault any thing where he is sure not to enter. He is not so well opinion'd of himselfe, as industrious to make other; and thinkes no uice so preiudiciall as blushing. Hee is still citing for himselfe, that a candle should not be hid under a bushell; and for his part, he will be sure not to hide his, though his candle be but a snuffe or Rush-candle. These few good parts he ha's, he is no niggard in displaying, and is like some needy flanting Gold-smith, nothing in the inner roome, but all on the cup-boord : If hee bee a scholler, he ha's commonly stept into the Pulpit before a degree ; yet into that too before he deseru'd it. Hee never deferres St Maries beyond his regencie, & his next Sermon is at Pauls Crosse, and that printed. He loves publike things a-life : & for any solemne entertainment he will find a mouth, find a speech who will. He is greedy of great acquaintance & many, & thinkes it no small advancement to rise to bee known. He is one that ha's all the great names at Court at his fingers ends, and their lodgings and with a sawcy My Lord will salute the best of them. His talke at the table like Beniamins messe, fiue times to his part, and no argument shuts him out for a quarrellour. Of all disgraces he indures not to be Non-plust and had rather flye for Sanctuary to Non-sense, which few can descry, then to nothing which all. His boldnesse is beholden to other mens modesty, which rescues him many times from a Baffle, yet his face is good Armour, and he is dasht out of any thing sooner then Countenance. Grosser conceits are puzzel'd in him for a rare man; and wiser men, though they know him, yet take him in for their pleasure, or as they would do a Sculler for being next at hand. Thus preferment at last stumbles on him, because he is still in the way. His Companions that flouted him before, now envy him, when they see him come ready for Scarlet, whilst themselves lye Musty in their old Clothes and Colledges.

65. A BAKER.

NO man verifies the Proverbe more, that it is an Almes-deed to punish him: for his penalty is a Dole, and do's the Beggers as much good as their Dinner. He abhorrs therefore workes of Charitie, and thinkes his Bread cast away when it is given to the poore. He loves not Iustice neither, for the weigh-scales sake, and hates the Clarke of the Market as his Executioner: yet hee findes mercy in his offences, and his Basket onely is sent to Prison. Marry a Pillory is his deadly enemy, and hee never heares well after.

66. A PRETENDER TO LEARNING.

IS one that would make all others more
fooles then himselfe ; for though he know
nothing, he would not have the world know
so much.   He conceits nothing in Learning
but the opinion, which he seekes to purchase
without it, though hee might with lesse
labour cure his ignorance, then hide it.   He
is indeed a kinde of Scholler-Mountebanke,
and his Art, our delusion.   He is trickt out
in all the accoutrements of Learning, and
at the first encounter none passes better.
He is oftner in his study, then at his Booke,
and you cannot pleasure him better, then
to deprehend him.   Yet he heares you not
til the third knocke, and then comes out
very angry, as interrupted.   You finde him
in his Slippers, and a Pen in his eare, in
which formality he was a sleep.   His Table
is spred wide with some Classick Folio, which
is as constant to it as the carpet, and hath
lain open in the same Page this halfe yeere.
His Candle is always a longer sitter up
then himselfe, and the boast of his Window
at Midnight, He walkes much alone in the
Posture of Meditation and ha's a Book still
before his face in the fields.   His pocket

is seldome without a Greeke Testament or Hebrew Bible, which he opens onely in the Church, and that when some stander by lookes over. He ha's sentences for Company, some scatterings of Seneca and Tacitus, which are good upon all occasions. If he read any thing in the morning, it comes up all at dinner : and as long as that lasts, the discourse is his. He is a great Plagiarie of Taverne-wit : and comes to Sermons onely that he may talke of Austin. His Parcels are the meere scrapings from Company, yet he complaines at parting what time he has lost. He is wondrously capricious to seeme a judgement, & listens with a sowre attention, to what he understands not : He talkes much of Scaliger and Causabone, and the Iesuites, and prefers some unheard of Dutch name before them all. He ha's verses to bring in upon these & these hints, & it shall goe hard but he will wind in his opportunity. He is criticall in a language he cannot conster, & speaks seldome under Arminius in Divinity. His businesse & retirement and caller away is his Study, and he protests no delight to it comparable. He is a great Nomenclator of Authors, which hee ha's read in generall in the Catalogue, and in particular in the Title, and goes seldome so farre as the

Dedication. Hee never talkes of any thing but learning, and learnes all from talking. Three incounters with the same men pumpe him, and then he onely puts in, or gravely sayes nothing. He ha's taken paines to be an Asse, though not to be a Scholler, and is at length discovered and laught at.

67. A POORE MAN

IS the most impotent man : though neither blind nor lame, as wanting the more necessary limmes of life, without which limmes are a burden. A man unfenc't and unsheltered from the gusts of the world, which blow all in upon him, like an un-rooft house : & the bitterest thing hee suffers, is his neighbours. All men put on to him a kind of churlisher fashion, and even more plausible natures churlish to him: as who are nothing advantag'd by his opinion. Whom men fall out with before-hand to prevent friendship, and his friends too, to prevent ingagements, or if they owne him, 'tis in private, & a by-roome, and on condition not to know them before company. All vice put together, is not halfe so scandalous, nor sets off our acquaintance further, and even those that are not friends for ends, doe not love any dearenesse with such men: The least courtesies are upbraided to him and himselfe thank't for none: but his best services suspected, as handsome sharking, and trickes to get money. And we shall observe it in knaves themselves, that your beggerliest knaves are the greatest, or thought so at least, for those that have witte to thrive by it, have art not to seeme so. Now a poore man has not vizard enough to maske his vices, nor ornament enough to set forth his vertues: but both are naked and unhandsome: and though no man is necessitated to more il, yet no mans ill is lesse excus'd but it is thought a kind of impudence in him to be vitious, and a presumption above his fortune. His good parts lye dead upon his hands, for want of matter to employ them, and at the best are not commended, but pittied, as vertues ill plac't and we say of him, 'Tis an honest man, but 'tis pitty: and yet those that call him so, will trust a knave before him. He is a man that ha's the truest speculation of the world, because all men shew to him in their plainest, and worst, as a man they have no plot on, by appearing good to: whereas rich men are entertaind with a more holly day behaviour, & see onely the best we can dissemble. He is the onely hee that tries the true strength of wisedome, what it can doe of it selfe without the helpe of fortune: that with a great deale of vertue conquers extremities, and with a great deale more his owne impatience, and obtaines of himself not to hate men.

68.   A HERALD

IS the Spawne, or indeed but the resultancy of Nobilitie, & to the making of him went not a Generation, but a Genealogie. His Trade is Honour, and he sells it, and gives Armes himselfe, though hee be no Gentleman. His Bribes are like those of a corrupt Iudge, for they are the prices of blood. Hee seemes very rich in discourse, for hee tels you of whole fields of Gold & Silver, O'r & Argent, worth much in French, but in English nothing. He is a greater diver in the streames or issues of Gentry, and not a by-Channell or Bastard escaps him, yea he do's with them like some shamelesse Queane, fathers more children on them, then ever they begot. His Trafficke is a kind of Pedlery-ware, Scutchions, and Pennons and little Daggers, and Lions, such as children esteeme and Gentlemen : but his pennyworths are rampant, for you may buy three whole Brawns cheaper then three Boares heads of him painted. He was sometimes the terrible Coat of Mars, but now for more mercifull Battels in the Tilt-yeard, where whosoever is victorious, the spoiles are his. He is an Art in England, but in Wales Nature, where they are borne with Heraldry in their mouthes, & each name is a Pedegree.

69. THE COMMON SINGING MEN

ARE a bad Society, and yet a company of good Fellowes, that roare deepe in the Quire, deeper in the Taverne. They are the eight parts of speech, which goe to the Syntaxis of Service, and, are distinguish't by their noyses much like Bells, for they make not a Consort, but a Peale. Their pastime or recreation is praiers, their exercise drinking, yet herein so religiously adicted that they serve God oftest when they are drunke. Their humanity is a legge to the Residencer, their learning a Chapter, for they learne it commonly before they read it, yet the old hebrew names are little beholden to them, for they mis-call them worse then one another. Though they never expound the Scripture, they handle it much, and pollute the Gospell with two things, their Conversation and their thumbes. Vpon worky dayes, they behave themselves at Prayers as at their pots, for they swallow them downe in an instant. Their Gownes are lac'd commonly with streamings of ale, the superfluities of a cup or throat above measure. Their skill in melody makes them the better companions abroad, and their Anthemes abler to sing Catches. Long liv'd for the most part they are not, especially the base, they over-flow their banke so oft to drowne the Organs. Briefly, if they escape arresting, they dye constantly in Gods Service; and to take their death with more patience, they have Wine and Cakes at their Funerall: & now they keepe the Church a great deale better, and helpe to fill it with their bones as before with their noyse.

70.   A SHOP-KEEPER.

HIS shop is his wel stuft Booke, and himselfe the Title-page of it, or Index. He vtters much to all men, though he sels but to a few, & intreats for his owne necessities, by asking others what they lacke. No man speakes more and no more, for his words are like his Wares, twenty of one sort, & he goes over them alike to all commers. He is an arrogant commender of his owne things;

for whatsoever hee shewes you, is the best in the Towne, though the worst in his shop. His Conscience was a thing, that would have layde upon his hands, and he was forc't to put it off: and makes great use of honesty to professe upon. He tels you lyes by rote, & not minding, as the Phrase to sell in, and the Language he spent most of his yeeres to learne. He never speakes so truely, as when he sayes he would use you as his Brother, for he would abuse his brother; & in his Shop, thinkes it lawfull. His Religion is much in the nature of his customers, and indeed the Pander to it: & by a mis-interpreted sense of Scripture makes a gaine of his godlinesse. He is your slave while you pay him ready money, but if hee once be-friend you, your Tyrant, and you had better deserve his hate then his trust.

71. A BLUNT MAN

IS one whose wit is better pointed then his behaviour, & that course, & impollisht not out of ignorance so much as humour. He is a great enemy to the fine Gentleman, and these things of Complement, and hates ceremony in conversations, as the Puritan in Religion. Hee distinguishes not betwixt faire and double-dealing, and suspects all smoothnes for the dresse of knavery. He starts at the encounter of a Salutation as an assault, and beseeches you in choller to forbeare your courtesie. He loves not any thing in Discourse that comes before the purpose, and is alwaies suspicious of a Preface. Himselfe falls rudely stil on his matter without any circumstance, except he use an old Proverbe for an introduction. He sweares old-out-of-date innocent othes, as by the Masse, by our Lady, and such like, and though there be Lords present, he cryes My Masters. Hee is exceedingly in love with his Humour, which makes him alwayes professe and proclaime it, and you must take what he sayes patiently, because hee is a plaine man. His nature is his excuse still, and other mens Tyrant: for he must speake his minde, and that is his worst, & craves your pardon most injuriously for not pardoning you. His Iests best become him, because they come from him rudely & unaffected: & he ha's the lucke commonly to have them famous. Hee is one that will doe more then hee will speake, & yet speake more then hee will heare: for though he love to touch others, he is touchy himselfe, and seldome to his owne abuses replyes but with his Fists. He is as squeazy of his commend-ations, as his courtesie, & his good word is like an Elogie in a Satyre. Hee is generally better favour'd then hee favours, as being commonly well expounded in his bitternesse, and no man speakes treason more securely. He chides great men with most boldnesse, and is counted for it an honest fellow. Hee is grumbling much in the behalfe of the Common-wealth, and is in prison oft for it with credit. He is generally honest, but more generally thought so, and his downe-rightnesse credits him, as a man not well bended and crookned to the times. In conclusion, he is not easily bad, in whom this quality is nature, but the counterfeit is most dangerous, since hee is disguis'd in a humour, that professes not to disguise.

72.   A HANDSOME HOSTESSE.

IS the fairer commendation of an Inne, above the faire Signe, or faire Lodgings : She is the Load-stone that attracts men of Iron, Gallants & Roarers, where they cleave sometimes long, and are not easily got off. Her Lipps are your wel-come, and your entertainement her company, which is put into the reckoning too, and is the dearest parcell in it : No Citizens wife is demurer then shee at the first greeting, nor drawes in her mouth with a chaster simper, but you may be more familiar without distaste, and shee do's not startle at Bawdry. She is the confusion of a Pottle of Sacke more then would have beene spent else-where, and her little Iugs are accepted to have her Kisse excuse them. She may be an honest woman, but is not beleev'd so in her Parish, and no man is greater a Infidell in it then her Husband.

73. A CRITICKE

IS one that ha's speld over a great many of Bookes, and his observation is the Orthographie. Hee is the Surgeon of old Authors, and heales the wounds of dust and ignorance. Hee converses much in fragments and Desunt multa's, and if hee piece it up with two Lines, hee is more proud of that Booke then the Author. Hee runnes over all Sciences to peruse their Syntaxis, & thinkes all Learning compris'd in writing Latine. Hee tastes Styles, as some discreeter Palats doe Wine ; and tels you which is Genuine, which Sophisticate & bastard. His owne phrase is a Miscellany of old words deceas'd long before the Cæsars, and entoomb'd by Varro, and the modern'st man hee followes, is Plautus. Hee writes Omneis at length, and quidquid, and his Gerund is most inconformable. Hee is a troublesome vexer of the dead, which after so long sparing must rise up to the Iudgement of his castigations. He is one that makes al Bookes sell dearer, whil'st he swells them into Folio's with his comments.

74.   A SERGEANT OR CATCH-POLE.

IS one of Gods Iudgements; and which our Roarers doe onely conceive terrible. Hee is the properest shape wherein they fancy Satan; for hee is at most but an Arrester, and Hell a Dungeon. Hee is the Creditors Hawke, wherewith they feaze upon flying Birds, & fetch them againe in his Tallons. He is the period of young Gentlemen, or their full stop, for when hee meets with them they can goe no farther. His Ambush is a Shop-Stall, or close Lane, and his Assault is cowardly at your backe. Hee respits you in no place but a Taverne, where hee sels his Minutes dearer then a Clock-maker. The common way to runne from him, is thorow him, which is often attempted and atchieved, and no man is more beaten out of Charity. He is one makes the streete more dangerous then the High-wayes, and men goe better provided in their walkes then their Iourney. Hee is the first handfell of the young Rapiers of the Templers : and they are as proud of his repulse, as an Hungarian of killing a Turke. He is a moveable Prison, & his hands two Manacles hard to bee fiel'd off. He is an occasioner of disloyall thoughts in the Common-wealth, for he makes men hate the Kings Name worse then the Devils.

75. AN ORDINARIE HONEST FELLOW

IS one whom it concernes to be call'd honest, for if hee were not this, he were nothing : and yet he is not this neither : But a good dull vicious fellow, that complyes well with the deboshments of the time, and is fitt for it : One that ha's no good part in him to offend his company, or make him to bee suspected a proud fellow : but is sociably a dunce, & sociably a drinker. That do's it faire & above boord without legerdemaine, & neither sharkes for a cup nor a reckoning. That is kinde or'e his beere, and protests hee loves you, and beginnes to you againe, and loves you againe. One that quarrells with no man, but for not pledging him, but takes all absurdities, and commits as many, and is no tell-tale next morning, though hee remember it. One that will fight for his friend if hee heare him abused, and his friend commonly is he that is most likely, & hee lifts up many a Iugge in his defence. Hee railes against none but censurers, against whom he thinkes hee railes lawfully, and censurers are all those that are better then himselfe. These good properties qualifie him for honesty enough, and raise him high in the Ale-house commendation, who, if he had any other good quality, would bee named by that. But now for refuge he is an honest man, and hereafter a sot : onely those that commend him, thinke not so, and those that commend him, are honest fellowes.

76. AN VNIVERSITIE DUNNE

IS a Gentlemans follower cheaply pur-chas'd, for his owne mony ha's hired him. Hee is an inferiour Creditor of some ten shillings or downewards, contracted for Horse-hire, or perchance for drinke, too weake to be put in Suite, & he arrests your modesty. Hee is now very expensive of his

time, for hee will waite upon your Staires
a whole Afternoone, and dance attendance
with more patience then a Gentleman-Vsher.
Hee is a sore beleaguerer of Chambers,
and assaults them sometimes with furious
knockes : yet findes strong resistance commonly, and is kept out. Hee is a great
complayner of Schollers loytering, for hee is
sure never to finde them within, & yet hee
is the chiefe cause many times that makes
them study. He grumbles at the ingratitude
of men, that shunne him for his kindenesse,
but indeed it is his owne fault, for hee is
too great an upbrayder. No man puts them
more to their braine then he; & by shifting
him off, they learne to shift in the world.
Some choose their roomes a purpose to
avoide his surprizals, and thinke the best
commodity in them his Prospect. He is
like a rejected acquaintance, hunts those
that care not for his company, and hee
knowes it well enough ; and it will not
keepe away.   The sole place to supple him,
is the Buttery, where hee takes grievous use
upon your Name, and hee is one much
wrought with good Beere and Rhetoricke.
Hee is a man of most unfortunate voyages,
and no Gallant walkes the streets to lesse
purpose.

77. A STAYED MAN

IS a man. One that ha's taken order with himselfe, & sets a rule to those lawlesnesses within him. Whose life is distinct and in Method, and his Actions as it were cast up before. Not loos'd into the Worlds vanities, but gathered up & contracted in his station. Not scatter'd into many pieces of businesses, but that one course hee takes, goe through with. A man firme and standing in his purposes, nor heav'd off with each winde and passion. That squares his expence to his Coffers, and makes the Totall first, and then the Items. One that thinkes what hee does, and does what he sayes, and foresees what hee may doe, before hee purposes. One whose (if I can) is more then anothers; assurance, and his doubtfull tale before some mens protestations. That is confident of nothing in futurity, yet his conjectures oft true Prophesies. That makes a pause still betwixt his eare and beleefe, and is not too hastly to say after others: One whose Tongue is strunge up like a Clocke til the time, and then strickes, and sayes much when hee talkes little. That can see the Truth betwixt two wranglers; and sees them agree even in that they fall out upon. That speakes no Rebellion in a bravery, or talkes bigge from the spirit of Sacke. A man coole and temperate in his passions, not easily betrai'd by his choller: That vies not oath with oath, nor heate with heat: but replies calmly to an angry man, and is too hard for him too. That can come fairely off from Captaines companies: and neither drinke nor quarrell. One whom no ill hunting sends home discontented, and makes him sweare at his dogs and family. One not hasty to pursue the new Fashion, nor yet affectedly true to his old round Breeches. But gravely handsome, and to his place, which suites him better then his Taylor; Active in the World without disquiet, and carefull without misery: yet neither ingulft in his pleasures, nor a seeker of businesse, but ha's his houre for both. A man that seldome laughs violently, but his mirth is a cheerefull looke. Of a compos'd & settled countenance, not set nor much alterable with sadnesse or joy. He affects nothing so wholly, that he must bee a miserable man when he loses it: but fore-thinks what will come hereafter, & spares Fortune his thankes & curses. One that loves his credit, not this word Reputation; yet can save both without a Duell: whose entertainements to greater

men are respectfull, not complementary, &
to his friends plaine, not rude. A good
Husband, Father, Master : that is without
doting, pampring, familiarity. A man well
poys'd in all humours, in whom nature
shewd most Geometry, & hee ha's not spoyl'd
the Worke. A man of more wisedome then
wittinesse, & braine then fancy ; and abler
to any thing then to make Verses.

78.   A SUSPITIOUS, OR IEALOUS MAN

IS one that watches himselfe a mischiefe,
and keepes a leare eye still, for feare it
should escape him. A man that sees a
great deale more in every thing then is to
be seene, & yet he thinkes he sees nothing:
His owne eye stands in his light. Hee is a
fellow commonly guilty of some weaknesses,
which he might conceale if hee were carelesse:
Now his over-diligence to hide them, makes
men pry the more. Howsoever hee imagines
you have found him, and it shall goe hard
but you must abuse him whether you wil
or no. Not a word can bee spoke, but nips
him somewhere: not a jest throwne out, but
he will make it hitt him ; You shall have
him goe fretting out of company, with some
twenty quarrels to every man, stung & gall'd,

and no man knowes lesse the occasion then
they that have given it. To laugh before
him is a dangerous matter, for it cannot
be at any thing, but at him, and to whisper
in his company plaine conspiracy. Hee
bids you speake out, and hee will answere
you, when you thought not of him : Hee
expostulates with you in passion, why you
should abuse him, and explaines to your
ignorance wherein, & gives you very good
reason, at last, to laugh at him hereafter.
He is one still accusing others when they
are not guilty, and defending himselfe, when
hee is not accused: & no man is undone more
with Apologies, wherein he is so elaborately
excessive, that none will beleeve him, and
he is never thought worse of, then when he
ha's given satisfaction : Such men can never
have friends, because they cannot trust so
farre : and this humour hath this infection
with it, it makes all men to them suspitious:
In conclusion, they are men alwayes in
offence & vexation with themselves & their
neighbours, wronging others in thinking
they would wrong them, and themselves
most of all, in thinking they deserve it.

FINIS.

www.ingramcontent.com/pod-product-compliance
Ingram Content Group UK Ltd.
Pitfield, Milton Keynes, MK11 3LW, UK
UKHW052101280225
455719UK00014B/453